RECUT MADNESS

by
JAMES FINN GARNER

FAVORITE
MOVIES RETOLD
FOR YOUR
PARTISAN
PLEASURE

THUNDER'S MOUTH PRESS
NEW YORK

RECUT MADNESS:
Favorite Movies Retold for Your Partisan Pleasure

Thunder's Mouth Press
An imprint of Avalon Publishing Group, Inc.
245 West 17th Street, 11th Floor
New York, NY 10011

Copyright © 2007 James Finn Garner

First Thunder's Mouth Press edition 2007

Library of Congress Cataloging-in-Publication Data is available.

ISBN-10: 1-56858-336-2
ISBN-13: 978-1-56858-336-5

9 8 7 6 5 4 3 2 1

Book design by Pauline Neuwirth, Neuwirth & Associates, Inc.

Printed in the United States of America
Distributed by Publishers Group West

To L, L, and L,
but especially L.

CONTENTS

INTRODUCTION

It's been said that a person's favorite movies can tell you something about their political leanings. Liberals, for instance, enjoy science fiction movies with multiracial casts and nonpolluting spaceships. Libertarians prefer more existential dramas, like noirish private eye flicks, Hitchcockian thrillers, and biographies of Ayn Rand. And conservatives? Conservatives simply love big, strapping cowboy movies. LoveloveloveloveLOVE them!

But why should art remain segregated? Why should a person's politics keep them from enjoying the full gamut of the cinematic arts? There's no reason a conservative voter shouldn't enjoy stories about rockets to other galaxies, as long as the space program is privately funded and its goal to evangelize the aliens clearly stated.

The technology exists today to let consumers send out their own radio podcasts, create music "mash-ups" with the best of Johnny Cash and 50 Cent, and copy and edit movies on their home computers. Why stop there? Why not allow consumers to rewrite, rethink, and recast classic films to reflect their political leanings? Why not let them enjoy what they can in a movie and shield themselves from anything that violates their deeply held preconceptions? If it can be done with the Bible, it can be done with *Boogie Nights*.

Recut Madness is an attempt to jump-start this process by reimagining classic films from a partisan frame of mind. This way, people living in blue states can unashamedly enjoy a war movie once in a while, and those in red states can enjoy a chick flick or surf comedy (but not a foreign film—there are limits to any idea, after all).

And perhaps beyond the pure entertainment value, these crossovers might serve a greater purpose. Perhaps they'll bridge the cultural divisions between us, inspire us to reconcile our differences, and help us all realize how much greater are the things that unite us.

Because it sure as shit ain't gonna happen in politics.

THE WIZARD OF DUBYA
(1939)

PART ONE

Kansas is a place of strong people and strong values. Out here, what's right is right and what's wrong is wrong. The people are hardworking, honest, and straightforward. In Kansas, life is good, the food is fresh and tasty, and there's plenty of room for everybody. Because everybody has moved away.

Out on the prairie on a small farm lives a young girl named Dorothy Gale. She's a bright, energetic, strapping girl who likes freedom and ponies and helping the less fortunate. Those who meet Dorothy for the first time might notice that for a girl of twelve, she's rather big for her age. Big, and amply endowed. Because of the steroids, hormones, and other feed supplements the family uses to make their livestock grow fat and meaty, Dorothy has physically matured well past her years. She masks this condition with youthful dresses of blue gingham, plus tight corsets and athletic bandages around her torso. For some boys and men, this camouflage only manages to fan the desires it was meant to thwart, but we'll let that story alone for the time being, while certain restraining orders are still in effect.

Dorothy lives on the farm with her Uncle Henry and Aunt Em, plus assorted hired hands, day laborers, hobos, drifters, and illegal "guest workers." It's honest, outdoor, union-free work, and the men are all glad to have it, and if they aren't, they can go back where they came from. (What's happened to Dorothy's parents, you might ask? Most likely they've been lured away by a decadent lifestyle somewhere on the coasts and are living selfish, hedonistic, miserable lives, while their daughter is growing up clear-eyed and buxom, working fourteen-hour days on this rundown but honest farm.)

Life isn't easy on Uncle Henry's farm. Winter hail, dust storms, and brush fires are common, and locusts are not unheard of. (Uncle Henry often says they call it "God's country" because it's where He likes to practice His favorite plagues, but he only says it when Aunt Em isn't around.) During lean times, they are too proud to look for a government handout. They believe in the maxim, "The Lord giveth and the Lord taketh away," and save their wrath for big-city grain speculators and the international Jewish banking cabal.

Dorothy's best friend is her dog Toto. His furry little face always makes her laugh, and he's a good listener for all her secrets. Like the time she took a wheelbarrow full of Uncle Henry's ammonium nitrate fertilizer and some blasting caps and gave that mean Jimmy Tolerud a birthday present he'd never forget. Dorothy doesn't have many secrets (the ones she does have are doozies), but it's still good to have Toto to confide in.

On the day our story begins, Toto has gotten Dorothy into trouble. She had been headed back home after a trip to town for a meeting of her Teen Empowerment Through Abstinence group (the title of the presentation was, "Take Hold of Your Future, but Keep Your Hands to Yourself"). Since there are no leash laws in their little slice of Eden yet, she lets Toto run free. The dog abuses this freedom, however, by digging up the garden of Miss Almira Gulch and, for good measure, taking a chomp out of her leg.

Throughout the county, Miss Gulch has a fearsome reputation, only part of which arises from her peculiar living arrangements with her old college roommate, known as Loretta. Dorothy and Toto are so scared they run back to the farm, where the girl tries to find anyone who will listen to her side of the story. But children are meant to be seen and not heard, even those who are freakishly tall and busty. Aunt Em tells her to find herself a place where she won't get into any trouble.

"Do you suppose there really is such a place, Toto? A place with no trouble? There must be, or else we wouldn't remember it and yearn for it. It's not a place you can get to with drugs or alcohol, but hard work and determination and no government interference. The way things used to be. Behind the moon, beyond the rain . . ."

SOMEWHERE OVER THE RAINBOW

Somewhere over the rainbow, way up high,
All the goods in the stores were made here, and not
    Shanghai.

Somewhere over the rainbow, time stands still
Life goes on as it always did and it always will.

I'd like to ride a time machine
To when our country's kids and teens
    Had school prayer,
With no quotas for sex or race,
    And everybody knows his place,
And is glad to stay there.

Somewhere over the rainbow, some folks say,
You can sing about rainbows and not imply you're gay.

And "gay" would mean "inclined to play,"
And not the way the gays mean "gay."

Before very long, Miss Gulch arrives at the farm, seeking satisfaction. This cold fish climbs off her bicycle, unbuckles her helmet, and unstraps her basket. She marches up to where everyone is standing.

"That dog is a menace to the community," Miss Gulch announces. "I've got an order from the sheriff to take him to the Fido Farms Canine Rehab Center, where he can get treatment to rechannel his aggressive urges. If you don't hand him over, I'll bring a damage suit and take your whole farm."

"That's just like your type," says Aunt Em, "with your tort lawyers and your big settlements. Someday the folks around here will train their own lawyers to change the laws to put *your* lawyers out of business, just to show some people still have *respect* for the *law*!"

More angry words are spoken, but Uncle Henry can see no way out. Over his niece's entreaties, he places Toto inside the bike basket. Dorothy runs into her room crying so hard she nearly splits her girdle.

"Almira Gulch," says Aunt Em courageously, "for twenty-three years, I've been dying to tell you what I thought of you! And now . . . well, being a *Christian* woman . . . I will!"

Following her statement comes twenty minutes of accusations, assumptions, innuendo, and outright insult that could've knocked the ears off a statue. Oh yes, Aunt Em is beginning to feel the spirit. When she starts speaking in tongues, Uncle Henry has to douse her with a pitcher of cold water and stand her in the corner by the hat rack.

"Since 'eating away at the moral fabric of the nation' takes so much time," Miss Gulch sniffs, "I'll be on my way." She attaches the basket with Toto inside to her bicycle.

"Late for softball practice?" Uncle Henry mutters, but only when she's out of earshot.

In her room, Dorothy cries and cries. In her corner, Aunt Em mumbles and shivers. In the shed, Uncle Henry takes a big swig of 'shine to calm his nerves. But down the road, brave little Toto will not be taken away so easily. He manages to open the lid to the basket, jumps from the moving bike, and runs home.

When her dog makes it back to the house, Dorothy's tears of sadness become tears of joy. But she knows Miss Gulch will return soon, so she must act quickly. Dorothy considers packing a suitcase and running away, but where could she possibly go that would be better than this hardscrabble little mudhole in the middle of nowhere? Dorothy weighs other options for dealing with Miss Gulch, only a few of which involve ammonium nitrate.

With all this going on in her head, Dorothy doesn't notice the weather, which is changing for the worse. A cold front moving in from the north is colliding with hot, moist air coming from the south. The conditions are perfect for a cyclone, a natural occurrence no matter what some pointy-headed climatologist with an agenda might want you to believe. As Dorothy goes out to the road to scope sites for booby traps, Toto becomes skittish from the coming storm and runs off into the cornfield. Dorothy chases after him.

Uncle Henry, the level-headed farmer, secures the horses and cows in the barn. Then, this stout yeoman of the soil puts Aunt Em under one arm and his jug of 'shine under the other, and carries them down to the storm cellar. He calls and calls for Dorothy but hears nothing but the shrill wind and the plaintive cries of the hired hands he's keeping away at gunpoint. Sadly, he heads into the cellar and closes the door.

Dorothy finds Toto and runs back into the house, which is swaying and shaking in the heavy wind. Dorothy takes Toto in her arms and asks, "Why, Toto? Why is God punishing us? That Miss Gulch is a mean old sinner—and everyone knows why she's been single all these years. That 'old college roommate' she lives with, she's butch enough to wallop Uncle Henry. Why doesn't God send the twister their way? Oh, I'm so confused!"

Just then, the window casing blows in and smacks Dorothy

on the head. She falls back as the house rocks on its foundation. All of a sudden, there's a massive crack, and the house is lifted into the air by the cyclone! Out of the window Dorothy can see all sorts of debris and double-wides blowing around and the land receding below.

The frightened girl runs to her bed and buries her face in the pillow, thinking of happy things like Christmas and the Constitution. Some time later, the twister weakens and the winds grow less fierce. Because housing can't stay sky-high forever, the farmhouse lands on the ground with a crash.

The sudden silence is almost as disturbing as the high winds had been. Dorothy walks to the door and cautiously steps out of the house. And what a sight does she behold! All around her, in unbearable contrast to the plain yet earnest Kansas landscape, is a world exploding with bright color. The trees, the plants, the flowers, even the grass! All are more beautiful and vibrant than she has ever imagined. This of course frightens her to death, so she sets off to do something about it.

continued on page 30

CHARLOTTE'S WEB

(2006)

BLUE STATE

It's a fine midsummer morning on Zucker-man's farm. The air is cool and sweet around the pigsty, as Wilbur stirs and rises from his manure pile. The recent weeks have been very busy, what with the newspaper reporters and the curious crowds who came to see the miracles on this farm.

Some time back, poor little Wilbur had been worried when he discovered he was being fattened to be slaughtered in the fall. He turned to his friend Charlotte the spider for help. Charlotte at the time calmed her friend and devised a shrewd plan to alert the humans that Wilbur was a very special swine. Her first effort was to weave a web in the barn doorway that spelled out "SOME PIG." This got attention from people for miles around, but eventually the excitement died down. To reinforce her message, she spun a second web that said "TERRIFIC." Surely, she thought, people were not so thick-headed that they would ignore two "miracles" and miss her message. Surley now they would understand.

So imagine Wilbur's shock on this fine morning when he hears Lurvy the farmhand say to Mr. Zuckerman, "He's a wonderful pig. You'll get some extra good ham and bacon when it comes time to kill that pig."

Wilbur ran crying and squealing, "Charlotte! Charlotte! They still want to kill me. I don't wanna die! I wanna live!"

"And live you shall," Charlotte says in her wise, calm voice.

For Charlotte knows something Wilbur doesn't: Zuckerman's farm is being targeted by the People for the *Really* Ethical Attention, Care & Handling of Animals (PREACHA). Having been tipped off by the wily spider, operatives from this group arrive that night, dressed in black like military commandos. They kidnap Mr. and Mrs. Zuckerman, as well as the fiendish Lurvy, and transport them to an unknown location. At dawn the next morning, Wilbur, Charlotte, and all the other animals find themselves on their own to run the farm. They are bewildered, to say the least, to find their pens open and no people to bring them their food.

"I'd thought I'd had the strangest dream," bleats the old sheep, "of a skinny man in a black leotard dancing through the mud and shouting 'Be free! Be free!' But I guess I wasn't asleep."

Wilbur says, "This is great! Now Zuckerman won't kill me for some cruel carnivore's breakfast."

"No-no-no, he won't," says the gander, "but now you can face-face-face the prospect of star-star-starving to death."

"You're right," says Wilbur fearfully. "We don't know anything about running a farm. What a catastrophe! Oh, what will we do?"

A deep voice answers him: "You know more than you think, and we can help you."

Wilbur turns to face two very large adult pigs, with concern in their eyes and smiles on their snouts. "Who are you?" Wilbur asks.

"Allow us to introduce ourselves. I'm Napoleon, and this is my comrade Snowball. We come from Manor Farm, down the road."

"Our farm is in the same situation as yours," Snowball says. "We've run the humans off, and now we're in control. This is an opportunity that we can use to help everybody—both your barnyard and ours."

"Gosh," says Wilbur.

"We'll go into more details after your farm is annexed," says Napoleon. "At that point, you'll be full and equal members in our farm, working toward a glorious future for animal-kind around the world!"

"Then," says Snowball confidentially, "you can help us locate another farm around these parts. We hear there's a pig around who thinks he's a sheepdog. Can you imagine? This 'Babe' character needs a strong talking to about ideological purity."

HIGH NOON

(1952)

Outside in the dusty, deserted street, the sun rises higher in the sky. Yet as it rises, the chances for a negotiated settlement continue to sink. In his office, the marshal sits, while the clock on his wall ominously ticks off the seconds until noon. The only other person in the room with the marshal is his yappy little deputy, the one with the bugged-out eyes and British accent. The marshal tries to ignore the bleatings from his deputy as he ponders recent developments, how he has come to be left alone to face danger.

He still finds it hard to believe: Had everyone in town really abandoned him at this crucial hour? Had everyone been so lacking in moral direction and fortitude that they only wanted to save their own skins? The threat was imminent, and the threat was real, and the threat was leaving there and coming over here on the noon train, and he was the only one who stood up and said "enough."

His former allies, the ones the marshal thought he could count on, all had their excuses for their inaction. Some said the danger was overstated. Others thought the peril could be talked away or contained or reasoned with. Others were simply tired of his hectoring them like schoolchildren. But he knew they were just cowards.

He remembers especially the fight with his fiancée. She just didn't understand why he had to put himself on the line. "Who knows how it will turn out? Have you given any thought to what will come later?" she'd asked.

"Well," he'd drawled in that New Englandy cowboy voice of his, "I can't wait for a smoking gun to turn into a mushroom cloud."

"I . . . I don't even know what that means," she'd said. And that was the last he heard from her.

So he's the last chance to bring hope to this town, to stand up to fear and tyranny, to dare to believe that people could live free.

"It's up to me," the marshal announces to the room. "A man's gotta do what a man's gotta do."

His deputy responds at length but says nothing, the marshal notices. The clock keeps ticking, closer and closer to noon.

"Some people said the best course would be to cut and run," the marshal says, "but if in the face of evil, you can't fight evil, then stopping evil is the last thing you try and do at the end."

The clock on the wall strikes noon. The marshal sets his jaw and walks out of the office. The train carrying his enemy will be arriving soon. The marshal stands in the street, his revolver ready (he'd decided he could get by without two). He is alone in the street as he hears the train arrive and depart. Then, around the corner by the livery stable, his enemy appears. To the marshal's surprise, he's brought some accomplices with him. About fourteen thousand of them.

The marshal gulps. He resists the urge to blame someone, although thoughts of his scouts, the telegraph operator, the newspaper publisher, and the previous marshal flash through his mind.

"History will vindicate me," he says to himself, over and over and over.

PULP FICTION
(1994)

In the sparsely furnished apartment, Brett—young and in way over his head—sits petrified, his neglected Big Kahuna Burger on the table in front of him. A silver automatic pistol, in the hands of hit man Jules Whitfield, is pointed at his clean-cut head. While threatening him, Jules regales him with knowledge of something his partner has just mentioned. "Hey, Brett, you know what they call a Quarter Pounder with Cheese in France? Do you? Tell 'em, Vincent."

From the kitchen, Vincent disinterestedly answers, "Royale with Cheese."

"You hear that?" sneers Jules. "Royale with Cheese. Now, that is some seriously f***ed up s**t. You know what the problem with that is? You know what the problem with that is?"

The terrified young man can hardly spit out, "W-w-w-what?"

"The metric system, that's what. What kind of a f***ed up system of measurement is it that forces you to call a hamburger a name by which it is unfamiliar? That's f***ed up."

Frustrated that Brett is missing his point, Jules turns and shoots Brett's friend who was lying on the couch. "Do I have your attention now?"

"Ai-ai-ai-yes! Yes!"

"See, that's how the French do it. They know that they're a second-rate country. They know the world is passing them by and leaving them in the dust. S**t, kids don't even learn French in school anymore. You take all the motherf***ers in this world who f***ing speak French, and all you end up with is Frenchmen, coupla Canadians, and some fancy-ass waiters up in Brentwood. And they're tryin' to tell *us* the way in which to refer to a Quarter Pounder? *Us*, the people who invented the hamburger itself? Aint' that some f***ed up s**t?"

"Y-y-y-y-y-y- . . ."

Jules shoots him in the shoulder. "Quit stuttering, it's getting on my nerves. Now tell me, ain't that f***ed up?"

"Yessir," he says through clenched teeth.

"Damn right it is. See, that's why we don't belong in the United Nations. Because the United Nations is the one place where this kind of s**t is tolerated. The United Nations is where France and all those other motherf***ers are allowed to f*** with our burgers. Now, what are you eating for breakfast there, Brett? Is that from McDonald's or Burger King?"

Brett can't believe his ears. "W-w-w-what?"

Jules levels his pistol and says, "Pay attention so I don't have to repeat myself."

"B-Big Kahuna Burger," he says, shuddering in pain.

"Big Kahuna Burger. I've heard of those. You mind if I have

a bite of your burger?" Jules picks up the sandwich and takes a bite. "See, now that's a damn tasty burger. With a good American name."

"It's a Hawaiian name," Vincent says.

"Which makes it an *American* name. Are you ignorant or what?"

"Now, Jules," says Vincent, "don't be startin'."

"Don't be startin' with *me*, Vincent."

"The United Nations don't want nothin' to do with hamburgers. They're all about wars and s**t."

"While I realize it's always fashionable and an easy laugh to make fun of the French, this doesn't alter the basic veracities which underpin my argument."

"So that's why we gotta send *you* to the UN as ambassador, right?"

"Right. To protect our burgers—and by extension, our entire culture. Don't you see, the hamburger is just a metaphor for the American way of life?"

Jules goes on at length about geopolitics until Vincent interrupts him. "See what you done? See what you done with all your talkin'? He's bled to death. Marsellus sends us here to do a job and make an impression, and you flap your gums so long the guy bleeds to death."

"Aw, motherf***er," Jules says, and begins to pump the body full of bullets. "How am I supposed to give my Ezekiel 27 speech to a goddamn corpse? Kid's got no idea about style."

And Brett is shot in a spray of crimson Technicolor beauty.

2001: A SPACE ODYSSEY
(1968)

RED STATE

In a harsh, rocky landscape, a tribe of hairy primates struggles for survival. They eat what they can pluck from trees or dig from the ground, or what they can scavenge from the kills of lions and panthers. They fight with hyenas over these scraps, as well as with hostile bands of their own kind, who often attack for food, for mates, for reasons unknown.

At night, the primates lie in fear, aware, in a way unique among the animals, that it is a dangerous world and that they are very vulnerable.

One particular morning, a male primate is idly toying with the bones of some carrion. A thigh bone fits snugly in his hand. Somehow, it feels good there.

The primate swings the femur one way and another. As he strikes, the other bones from the carcass break into shards. Pieces fly. The slight inkling of an idea erupts somewhere in his brain, and he has visions of himself in slow motion using the bone as a hunting tool and a weapon.

Suddenly there is noisy confusion everywhere. His tribe runs to him, followed by a marauding pack of other primates. They circle round defensively, and shriek in anger and fear.

The primate with the bone raises it high in the air. He is confident now his tribe will have an edge in the fight for survival. As he holds it aloft, a bolt of flame erupts from the distance, knocking the bone from his hand. He shrieks in pain, while the other primates hoot and cower. From over a small hill comes the archangel Michael and a dozen other heavenly soldiers. They're followed by a pink-skinned man and woman, riding together on a majestic triceratops.

All the primates huddle together, shaking and screeching. The archangel says, "You were right, Adam, there was a tribe of *Afarensis* out here." Raising his fiery sword to the sky, he proclaims, "All right, monkey boys, in the name of the Lord Almighty, prepare to get fossilized!"

"Adam," the pink-skinned woman says to her partner, "why are we doing this again?"

"To thwart intellectual vanity among academic eggheads, of course."

"Oh," she says. "I see. And they are who, exactly?"

Adam gives her a look that tells her further questions would be unseemly.

At this point, one angel tosses his sword into the sky, where it revolves end over end in slow motion, until we reach the present day, and it turns into a Star Wars Missile Defense Shield satellite.

THE GRADUATE

(1967)

A *party is* being thrown at the bourgeois Braddock house for their son Benjamin, who recently graduated from college. Tentative at the prospect of his future, Benjamin is being assaulted by the tipsy, middle-aged friends of his parents, who are telling him what he should look forward to in his life. One man, Mr. McGuire, is walking with Benjamin alongside the backyard pool. "Ben," he says confidentially, "I just want to say one word to you, just one word . . ."

"Yessir," says Benjamin.

The pool lights shine up, lending eerie tones to their faces. "Are you listening?"

"Yes, I am," says Benjamin earnestly.

Mr. McGuire lowers his voice and says gravely, "Plastics."

There is a long pause before Benjamin asks, "Exactly how do you mean?"

"There's a great future in plastics. Biodegradable, even edible, made from switchgrass and marsh sorghum. Oh, and biomass energy extraction. And aquatic ranching. Those three."

"I see."

"Or iPod accessories. Big market in that. Think about it. Will you think about it?"

"Yes, I will," says Benjamin.

TRIUMPH OF THE WILL

(1935)

BLUE STATE, WITH RED ON THE FRINGE

This marvelous documentary/travelogue opens with thrilling aerial shots aboard a Junker-52, flying like an eagle through billowing, majestic clouds. You can almost feel yourself piloting the airplane through the sky—or flying yourself, like some sort of superman! The images of clean white clouds are wonderfully soothing. The worries of the world can't reach you up here. Soon, you're feeling young and carefree for the start of your Bavarian holiday.

In moments, the landscape comes into view, and you see the majestic old city of Nuremburg. Church spires, castle towers, picturesque bridges with parades marching across them. The kind of city you might find in a fairy tale. Your small plane touches down in an airfield, and what a sight greets you! Hundreds of smiling happy faces, young and old, so excited to welcome new visitors. They all raise their hands in unison to hail you, as if they've been practicing it for just this occasion. Like you are the only guest they've got their eyes on.

You take a car into the ancient city. The streets are lined with local people, all waving and smiling and thrilled to see you. Some even lean from the upper windows of their houses to shout their greetings! Chubby-cheeked children, old hausfraus with their hair in braids, young ladies waving handkerchiefs— all intent on showing you good old-fashioned Bavarian hospitality. You check in to your hotel, the Hotel Deutscher Hof, tired but exhilarated as you think about what the next day will bring. Your only care is whether the marching bands in the courtyard and the people carrying torches and starting bonfires will eventually stop so you can get some rest.

The view from your hotel window the next morning is a frozen glimpse of history. Tiled rooftops, puffing chimneys, and old towers in the morning mist hearken back to another time, a more glorious era. It promises to be a gorgeous day to spend outside as you ride to the outskirts of town. These folks sure do love the outdoors—look at all those campsites! Row upon row, and all neat as a pin. Armies of healthy young men shave and do their morning wash-ups at steel troughs—boy, that water looks cold!—but they can't stop themselves from a little horseplay. Boxing, wrestling, piggyback rides, blanket toss—thank heaven these boys have an outlet for their energy. All that activity builds up an appetite, and luckily the camp cooks have been up for hours making coffee, potatoes, and oatmeal. Look at those tasty strings of sausages, all handmade and all kosher.

Later in the morning, it's parade time on the festival grounds! Folk dancers in elaborate native costumes bring the heritage of ancient Bavaria to life. Horse riders in funny safety helmets command their steeds in a show of strength and finesse. Young blond boys bang drums for their marching bands with deadly serious looks on their angelic faces. And what's this? A precision shoveling team? Ha ha, only in Bavaria!

And then, to demonstrate their intense focus on hospitality and *gemütlichkeit*, an entire stadium of people stand silently as leader after uniformed leader speaks in a montage at the podium:

> We . . . welcome the esteemed representatives of the foreign countries, . . . in sincere friendship. . . . Wherever one looks, construction is in progress, improvements are being made, and new values created. . . . Today we are all working together, in the bogs, quarries, in the sandpits, on the dikes of the North Sea. . . . Fields and forests, acres and bread—Let's . . . glorious . . . ly . . . party!
>
> It is better and more gratifying to win the heart of a nation and keep it. . . . Only a lunatic or a deliberate liar could think . . . otherwise. . . . A nation that does not value its . . . comrades . . . will perish. . . .
>
> The German people are happy . . . to serve . . . you . . . and . . . wait solely for your order and your order alone. . . . What is bad, has no place among us! . . . (applause) Again and again, people will come and go, they will be moved anew, be pleased and equally inspired, because . . . You are not dead, you are alive—in Germany!

Their passion is so strong, they are practically shouting their friendly message. An involuntary chill runs down your spine.

These are scenes you'll never be able to forget, long after the last fireworks have exploded, the last bonfire has burned out, and the last chants of "Hi! Hi! Hi!" have stopped echoing in your ears.

NETWORK

(1976)

RED STATE

"*I don't want* you to protest. I don't want you to riot. I don't want you to write your congressmen, because I wouldn't know what to tell you to write. I don't know what to do about the depression and the inflation and the Russians and the crime in the street. All I know is, first you've got to get *mad*. You've got to say: 'I'm a human being, *goddammit. My life has value.*'"

The angry, rain-wet face of Howard Beale is shown on monitors throughout the control room, as well as TV screens in homes around the country.

"So I want you to get up now," he pleads. "I want all of you to get up out of your chairs. I want you to get up right now, go to the window, open it, and stick your head out and yell: 'I'm mad as hell and I'm not going to take this anymore!'"

The scene cuts to a panel discussion. "Wow," laughs Jack McCracken, host of the cable show *Fill Me In, with Jack McCracken*. "Looks like someone should switch to decaf. Dick

Middleton, your thoughts on Howard's little tirade here? Is he passionate, or just insane?"

"This just goes to show that the Democrat Party is out of ideas," says Dick Middleton of the Free Heritage Enterprise Freedom Institute. "Look, he tells you right in the beginning: They don't know what to do about crime in the streets. They don't have any new ideas about how to deal with the Russians, and by extension, any other country in the world. They don't know what to do about the depression—a depression, I might point out, that had its roots in the last Democrat administration seven years ago. So in absence of all that, they just come on TV all foaming at the mouth."

"We're still wiping off the cameras," McCracken chuckles.

"And while he didn't mention his party affiliation in his rant there, Howard Beale works in the media, ergo he is a Democrat."

"Sound Aristotelian logic there. You intellectuals at the think tanks keep us on our toes. Anne Reksik, anything more to add?"

"Where do you start commenting on this?" says Anne Reksik, a regular commentator on *Fill Me In*. "It looks like the bus just arrived from Crazytown, and Howard Beale's in the driver's seat."

"Why do you think he's so angry here?" McCracken asks.

"Obviously, with the Democrats out in the political wilderness, Howling Howard hasn't been able to slake his thirst for Filipino rent boys and methamphetamine."

"Those are serious charges," says the host, "but I won't argue with you. Viewers should go to our Web site and join in tonight's click poll: 'Howard Beale: Lunatic or Crackpot?' Let your voice be heard.

"Coming up after the break, we'll discuss democracy and the consolidation of the press. Will fairer media ownership rules allow a more vigorous public debate? Joining me will be Dick Middleton, author of the new book, *When I Want Your Opinion, I'll Beat It Out of You*, and Anne Reksik, newly appointed director of the Voice of America. Back after these messages for mechanical adjustable beds."

FULL METAL JACKET

(1987)

BLUE STATE

In the barracks that night, the recruits are lined up in front of their bunks at attention. They are nervous young men, clad in their white, government-issued underwear. They are ready to be turned into whatever the drill sergeant wants them to be. Drill Sergeant Hartman surveys the group. He puts his hands behind his back, paces down the aisle, and addresses them gruffly.

"Tonight," he bellows, "you pukes will sleep with your rifles! You will give your rifle a girl's name! Not because women are objects of death and destruction, but because you need to learn a little respect! You will treat this rifle with tenderness and affection. You are married to this piece, this weapon of iron and wood! And you will be faithful! And then maybe—just *maybe!*—you can move up to respecting your fellow men and women in the world. Port . . . hut! Prepare to mount! *Mount!*"

The recruits mount their bunks at this command, and lay on their backs with their arms at attention. A few of them, it's safe to say, are a little excited about what is to come.

"Port . . . hut!" shouts the drill sergeant. The recruits snap their rifles to the port arms position over their chests. "Now . . . tell me *how you feel!*"

"This is my rifle," the recruits chant in unison. "There are many like it, but this one is mine. My rifle is my best friend, which is kind of sad, but I am working hard at my skills in the interpersonal relationship department and hope to improve soon.

"Anyway, this is my rifle, a weapon of masculine aggression that I will use strictly in self-defense, and then, only grudgingly. I will at all times try and disperse hostility, avoid conflict, and negotiate a settlement, even at my own expense, until everyone is satisfied with the outcome. At that point, I will begin to work my way out of my job as peacekeeper, so that my experience and effort can be forgotten, and I can begin some really useful work, like tutoring.

"There may be others who wish to kill me, but that doesn't give me the imperative or the right to kill them, and besides, shouldn't my moral example count for something? And so I will march on, until wars are not needed and mankind enters a new era of consciousness and compassion."

Satisfied, Drill Sergeant Hartman says, "Order . . . hut!" And the recruits snap their rifles down to their sides. "At ease!" As he turns off the barracks lights, he says, "Good night, ladies."

The recruits from the bunks shout in reply, "Good night, sir! Sweet dreams, sir!"

THE WIZARD OF DUBYA

(1939)

PART TWO

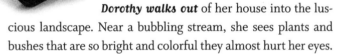

Dorothy walks out of her house into the luscious landscape. Near a bubbling stream, she sees plants and bushes that are so bright and colorful they almost hurt her eyes.

"What is this place, Toto? Are we really over the rainbow? Or is this some kind of new theme park?"

While Dorothy marvels at all this luscious greenery, Toto goes nearly berserk, sniffing the smells of unknown critters and frantically marking his own territory. Soon, he starts to bark excitedly. Dorothy hears sounds, too, like a whine off in the distance, like you might hear from a flock of noisy birds. It grows louder and louder, until Dorothy feels she can hear voices in the din. She nearly jumps out of her skin as crowds of people—itty-bitty people no higher than her waist—approach her on paths from every side. Some of them are carrying signs, others sticks and hoes and flags. Strangest of all, the mobs seem to be either of two groups, and, depending on affiliation, are dressed completely in red or blue.

When the mobs set their eyes on Dorothy, their jaws drop open. They approach her from both sides cautiously. Despite their childlike stature, their faces are old and wrinkled. Dorothy wonders if maybe she has indeed landed in a theme park, because it's beginning to feel a lot like Florida.

One of the little people, dressed in blue, edges up to her and asks in a very high voice, "What are you doing here?"

"I don't know," she answers.

"Well then, which side are you on?"

"I don't know that, either."

"Do you expect us to believe that?" peeps someone from the red-clad mob. "Why would you build this squatter's shack if you weren't trying to undermine property rights?"

Someone from the other side yells, "Why would she build here if she wasn't a friend of the tufted titmouse?"

"But I . . ."

"Why do you despise landowners?" shouts the crowd to one side.

"Why do you hate nature?" shouts the other.

"I can't . . ." Dorothy stutters.

"Tell us! Tell us! Tell us! Tell us!"

"Can't you let me think for a minute?"

"Hell NO!" they answer. The shouts and the rants from the little people grow and grow until a person can't tell them apart. The noise becomes so loud—like a hundred teakettles whistling at once—Dorothy has to plug her ears. Finally, to get their attention, she grabs some of their little picket signs and throws them on the ground, then whistles loudly with her fingers the way Uncle Henry had taught her.

"Now, what's so important that you people are at each other's throats?" she asks.

"This land is the site of a new housing development," says one man proudly. "The Estates of Munchkin Glen Commons. Gorgeous three-kitchen, ten-bath houses on spacious lots, each of which backs up onto an eighteen-hole golf course."

"Golf course?" Dorothy asks.

"Well," he admits, "minigolf."

Another Munchkin interrupts, "But this is the habitat of the tufted titmouse, the titted tuftmouse, the mousey tuft-tit, and other endangered birds and animals with even cuter names. You can't build it here! They'll become extinct!"

The developer counters, "Hey, stuff goes extinct all the time, but how often does a real estate opportunity like *this* come down the pike?"

Another shouts, "And hiring a giant to come and build a shack doesn't change things, no matter *how* stacked she is."

"Enough of this!" Dorothy yells. "I need to make it clear: I didn't *build* my house here. My house *flew* here from far away."

"Outside agitators!" shouts someone in the crowd.

"No, listen, please. My house was picked up in a tornado and thrown through the sky. Somehow it was dropped down right here." She begins to walk toward the house, hoping to figure out a way to calm these creatures. "You see, Toto and I came from our farm, back in Kansas. Have you ever heard of Kansas? You'd love it. Why, it's full of the most honest and hardworking—EEEEK!!"

As Dorothy turns the corner, she faces a sight that makes her blood run cold. Sticking out from under a corner of her house are two legs, human-sized, wearing red striped stockings and sparkling ruby slippers.

One mutters, "Strange taste in gardening you've got."

"What do you know from gardening?" says another. "You were once engaged to a garden gnome, as I recall."

"This isn't my garden," Dorothy says. "My house dropped down here and landed on this poor woman."

"This poor woman?" scoffs a red Munchkin. "Bah! It's the Wicked Witch of the East. She deserved to snuff it."

"Oh, did the witch do bad things?" asks Dorothy.

"Oh, terrible things."

"Like what?"

"She . . . she was wicked, y'know? You could never tell with her. She was always . . . about to do something wicked. That's what witches do. They wouldn't call her the Wicked Witch if she weren't wicked, would they? Doing witchy-type things, wickedly?"

"But you nailed her," says a red Munchkin. "A preemptive strike!"

The Red Munchkins all let out a cheer. "Hooray! No coddling of witches here!"

One of the Blue Munchkins shouts out, "This is a terrible safety hazard. We need tighter controls on falling houses."

Half of the crowd voices its agreement, while the other half bellows its disagreement.

"Falling houses don't kill people," one shouts. "People kill people."

"Yeah, when they drop houses on 'em!"

Dorothy doesn't know what to do. The bickering noise is driving her crazy, Toto is barking left and right, and her little house is now a crime scene. If she ever thought that her life back in Kansas lacked excitement, she has plenty of it now. And it's plenty weird.

Just then, over the tops of the little houses and the psychedelic landscape floats a small silver bubble. It's hard to notice at first, but it grows and grows and makes ever-louder tinkly sounds. The bickering dies down, as all of the Munchkins begin to watch the bubble and coo in amazement. They're easily distracted, apparently, by shiny objects.

Soon the bubble alights and disappears, and in its place stands a beautiful woman dressed in layers of white organza and crinoline. She wears a tall crown, above which wiggle small white stars attached to fine wires. She beams a calm, happy smile at everyone. Dorothy can't help but like her, even after she realizes that the woman's smile never relaxes and her eyes never focus on anything. And that some of the stars floating around her head aren't really attached.

"Are you a good witch," the woman asks in a high, quivery voice, "or a bad witch?"

Dorothy is shocked by the question. "Neither one," she says. "I'm an independent."

"I'm Glinda, the Witch of the North," the frilly woman chirps. "I'm also president of the Concerned Witches of Munchkinland and the Twenty-first Century Bubble Project. Because, 'Life in a bubble eliminates trouble.' That's our motto, you see."

"I'm Dorothy Gale, of Kansas," she curtsies.

"How old are you, Dorothy?"

"Twelve."

"You're quite . . . healthy for a girl of twelve." Glinda waves her wand, and suddenly the sleeves of Dorothy's dress grow longer, and her hem lowers nearly to her ankles. "Just to discourage any ideas among the male Munchkins. They can stick their noses into some of the most untoward places, believe me."

"So, you're a good witch?" Dorothy asked.

"More like a holier-than-thou witch," one of the Munchkins grumbles.

There's a slight droop in the corner of Glinda's smile, and a twitch in her right eye, but otherwise she ignores this. "If you are not a witch, then is *that* the witch?"

"Toto? Toto's my dog."

"Listen, my child," says the witch confidentially as she pulls Dorothy aside, "you obviously don't know the first thing about witch hunts. This crowd's out for blood, so if you want to save your hide, you'd better find someone else to fill the bill, like your four-legged buddy there."

"How can you say that?" Dorothy cries, hugging the dog in her arms. "Poor little thing didn't hurt anybody."

"I received an anonymous tip that a new witch had just dropped a house on the Wicked Witch of the East. And there's the house, and here you are, and there he is, and there they are, and there's where they keep the torches and pitchforks, and that's all that's left of the Wicked Witch of the East."

Dorothy turns to look at the legs sticking out from under her house. Again she feels a chill go through her body. "But if she was such a bad witch, shouldn't they be happy she's gone?"

"Ah, you'd think so, but," shrugs the witch in white, "mob psychology. What can you do?"

When Glinda asks the little people whether they're glad the Wicked Witch is gone, they shout out many things. Some say strong leaders are always misunderstood, and history would vindicate her. Some fiery types say they're sorry she escaped Munchkin justice, which is swift and cruel and relies heavily on what's known as the "falsetto method." Some worry that without a strong leader, Munchkinland will soon be overrun by the armies of their enemies, such as the Winkies and the Growleywogs (which are both vicious, bloodthirsty societies, despite their cute names).

"So you see, my dear," smiles the Witch, "they all love Munchkinland so much, they'd happily burn it to the ground to save it."

"I've never seen people like this before," Dorothy says.

"There used to be Munchkins of all colors and shapes. Now there are only the red and the blue, and both are equally rabid. I blame the coffee."

Dorothy just shakes her head in disbelief at the jabbering crowd.

"Wait a minute!" pipes up one Munchkin with a heavily lacquered goatee. "How do we know she's really dead?"

"Whaddya mean, 'How do we know?'" says a young tough wielding a giant lollipop with menace. "She had a frickin' *house* dropped on her!"

"Well, how can we be sure?"

Another says, "Yeah, how can we be so quick to pull the plug on her? Maybe under all that clapboard, part of her is still clinging to life."

"The crushed part, or the mangled part?" the young tough asks.

"From this distance," says the one with the goatee, peering toward the house, "I detect some signs of life. And as long as one casual, untrained, loud-mouthed, buttinski observer has questions about whether she's dead, we have to give her the benefit of the doubt."

"Where's the coroner?" someone shouts. "We need one of them huge Certificates of Death!"

From the hooting crowd emerges a sober-looking Munchkin dressed all in black, wearing a hat the size of a small canoe. He dutifully unrolls an official-looking scroll with "Certificate of Death" printed at the top, and begins to sing in a strange warble:

As coroner, I must aver,
I've thoroughly examined her.
Her head, this shack did bash it in.
I do assert, she's cashed it in.

In most places, a coroner's report so beautifully gargled would be an end to the matter. But here in Munchkinland, where right is right, only incredibly more so, there are protests and counterprotests, vigils and countervigils, an inquiry into the coroner's credentials, death threats, bomb scares, and a petition to hold a recall election. Dorothy observes that, as much as these little people fear wicked witches, Winkies, and Growleywogs, they fear each other even more.

Suddenly in the middle of the bickering crowd erupts a cloud of blue, oily smoke. The Munchkins scatter. Out of the cloud come two large men wearing black suits, earpieces, and opaque sunglasses. When they are satisfied the site is secure, they adjust their ties and step back. Following them from the cloud is a blond woman in a gray business suit. As she emerges, her expression changes from a chilling aggressive scowl to an even more chilling smile. While a few Munchkins warm to her presence, most of the others scurry as if from a rabid dog.

"Who's that?" Dorothy asks.

"That, my dear, is the Wicked Witch of the Northeast," Glinda says unpleasantly, "although the carpetbagger only moved there because another witch was retiring."

"She's wicked, too? Gee, she seems so nice, so concerned."

"She's only concerned to the point where she gains power from it," Glinda says with a brittle sneer. "She wants to control people's lives and set up a socialist 'mommy' state."

"So, she's not really concerned?"

"No, child, not *genuinely*," Glinda smiles condescendingly. "Not like the *rest* of us witches."

"She's pretty," says Dorothy, "but how does she get her hairstyle to change every few seconds like that?"

A red Munchkin nearby adds, "Can you believe it? The Witch of the Northeast wants to make sure everyone has health care. Insanity! Have you ever seen a fitter, healthier bunch of people than us?" The bandy-legged little bald man slaps his potbelly in contentment and immediately ruptures his appendix.

The Wicked Witch of the Northeast moves through the crowd, patting heads, pinching cheeks, even hoisting two or three Munchkins at a time for hugs. Working her way toward the wreck of Dorothy's house, she puts a hand to her chest and says, "Oh, what a tragedy. It is unconscionable that the families of Munchkinland should have to endure this."

Glinda says, "Oh, really?"

"Glinda," says the other, "we've had our differences in the past, but it's time to pull together in this time of sorrow."

"My dear, you are as bad an actor as you ever were. Besides, there are no cameras here yet."

The expression on her face changes, and the Wicked Witch of the Northeast growls, "I was *told* there'd be a photo op here." Pausing a moment, she dials a number on her cell phone and fires three assistants. She snaps the phone shut and says in a steely tone, "All right then, I'll just take what I came for and jet out."

The Wicked Witch walks over to the house in her sensible shoes and without emotion stands by the legs of her fallen sister. As she reaches down to take the ruby slippers, however, they disappear.

"Aaaaggghhh! What have you done with them?" she shouts. "I've put in my time, I deserve to have them!"

"Too late," Glinda says. She points her wand downward, and Dorothy sees that the ruby slippers are now on her own feet, magically neat and snug. "There they are, and there they'll stay."

"Give them to me. You don't have the security clearance to use them."

"Keep tight inside of them," Glinda warns Dorothy. "Their magic must be very powerful, or else this power-crazed, tax-and-spend, abortion-on-demand, cuckolded, socialist she-male wouldn't want them."

Though still as wrathful as her name would imply, the Wicked Witch of the Northeast grows calm. And the calmer she gets, the scarier she becomes. "All right, you've won this time. You and your vast conspiracy are quite effective. But I'll get you, my pretty, and your little dog, too." And with that, she retreats into the billowing cloud of blue smoke, along with her security contingent, and disappears.

"My, my," Glinda says. "How unladylike. It seems you've made quite an enemy. And I fear she will try and make good on her threats."

"Oh! Then Toto and I have to get back to Kansas right away. How can we get there?"

Glinda shakes her starry head. "To the east and west of Munchkinland are vast deserts. To the north is the Great Sandy Waste. And to the south is someplace with lots of poor people. I'm afraid you're hemmed in on all sides."

This awful news makes Dorothy feel like crying. "What am I going to do? Isn't there anyone who can help me?"

"There is one person who might know . . . the Wizard of Dubya."

"Is he a good wizard?"

Before Glinda can answer, the Munchkins begin shouting things like "Genius! Idiot! Patriot! Crook!" It seems like no two Munchkins hold the same opinion of the Wizard and as always are ready to fight about it.

"Quiet, please, quiet!" shouts the witch, raising her fingers to her dainty temple. "The Wizard is . . . complicated, but he's got power. If anyone can get you back to Kansas, it is he. It won't be free or painless, of course, because as he says, 'Somethin' is nothin' you can make without somethin'.' Please, don't ask me to explain such sublime wisdom. The Wizard lives in the Emerald City, which is many days' journey from here."

Dorothy asks, "How do I get to the Emerald City?"

Glinda chirps with a frozen smile, "Just follow the Yellow Brick Road."

Dorothy looks down where Glinda is pointing, but she sees no yellow bricks. In fact, it can hardly be called a road. It's more of a ripped up path or gully, paved in part with wooden planks and an occasional yellow-painted cinderblock every few feet. A few yards off, a large sign reads:

SAFER BRICK ROAD INITIATIVE
We appreciate your inconvenience and
are right there with ya.
DEPT. OF TRAFFIC ENHANCEMENT,
IN PARTNERSHIP WITH THE STONE-JENKINS CORPORATION.
The Wizard

Dorothy turns to ask another question, but Glinda is already in her bubble, floating head over heels above the crowd, waving slowly and talking to herself as she drifts away. As if by signal, all the Munchkins surround Dorothy and begin a fresh, harmonic harangue.

Follow the Yellow Brick Road,
Follow the Yellow Brick Road,
Short a brick or two, but we'll pull through,
Follow the Yellow Brick Road.

And before she can object or ask questions or even get a bite to eat, Dorothy is whirled down the disassembled Yellow Brick Road by the manic energy of the Red and Blue Munchkins. She has to skip and leap carefully so as not to trip on the road's wreckage or twist her ankle in a hole. The Red Munchkins sing:

You're off to see the Wizard,
The Wonderful Wizard of Dubya!
Strong and fair, we know he cares,
Don't let anything trouble ya.
Don't you misunderestimate,
The Wizard of Dubya's really great,
Really really really really great!
We're lucky to have him controlling our fate!
You're off to see the Wizard!
The Wonderful Wizard of Dubya!

Then the Blue Munchkins sing their rejoinder:

You're off to see the Wizard,
The Wonderful Wizard of Dubya!
Dumb as a post, sharp as pot roast,
If you come empty-handed, he'll snub ya.

If ever you hated a potentate,
The Wizard of Dubya is one to hate,
Berate, deflate, abate, debate, negate!
If only that lightweight would abdicate!
You're off to see the Wizard!
The Wonderful Wizard of Dubya!

Spinning and swirling, the Munchkins waltz her all the way to the entrance to their gated community, wish her well, and slam the door, glad that she and her dog are now someone else's problem.

continued on page 68

IT'S A WONDERFUL LIFE
(1946)

RED STATE, AFFLUENT SUBURB

It's a cold damp morning, the streets filled with ice and slush that apparently no one feels obliged to shovel. Just the sort of morning that would aggravate Henry Potter's arthritis and set him into a foul mood for the day. He arrives early at the bank where he is president, for indeed he has no other place to go. As Maurice wheels him into the bank, several of the sycophants who work there come up to say good morning. "As if they believe in things like Christmas bonuses," Potter thinks to himself.

When this bunch disperses, Potter is accosted by that rumpled clown from the Bailey Building & Loan. One of his nephews was being awarded the Medal of Honor that day, and Uncle Billy Bailey feels obliged to rub his exuberant pride into the face of a sick, lonely man in considerable pain. Roughly grabbing the newspaper out of Potter's hand, Bailey mocks him mercilessly as he reads the headline.

"Well, good morning, Mr. Potter. What's the news? Well,

well, well, 'Harry Bailey Wins Congressional Medal.' That couldn't be one of the Bailey boys? You just can't keep those Baileys down, now, can you, Mr. Potter?"

He can smell the liquor on Bailey's breath. Trying to remain professional, Potter says, "How does slacker George feel about that?"

"Very jealous, very jealous," says Bailey. "He only lost three buttons off his vest. Of course, slacker George would have gotten two of those medals if he had gone."

Bailey gives him back his paper, as Potter tries to get away and attend to business. The inebriate, however, hurls one more taunt at the old man. "After all, Potter, some people like George had to stay home. Not every heel was in Germany and Japan!"

Once inside his office, Potter unfolds his newspaper and is surprised to find an envelope—an envelope stuffed with cash. This is not the first secret envelope he has ever been slipped, nor slipped to another, so he keeps his calm. At his desk, he opens the bulging envelope and counts out $8,000 in medium-sized bills.

Potter wipes his mouth in thought. Is this some kind of bribe? He's been leaning on the Baileys fairly strongly of late. The end of the war might mean the end of an opportunity for scuttling their business and consolidating the town's banking assets in an efficient way. Bribery didn't seem to be a method the Baileys would use, but who knew? That daffy old man might have been hiding a keen intelligence and ruthlessness under his unthreatening appearance. "Uncle Billy Bailey," indeed. Who would suspect someone with a childish name like that?

If this is in fact a bribe, what is the best thing to do? Should he take it, and be complicit in whatever plan they are hatching, or should he report it to the banking authorities? Was the $8,000 worth more in hand or in future business taken from the Baileys? They are not to be trusted, this much he knows, but what could their angle possibly be?

These questions tear at Potter until sweat forms on his brow. For the first time in many, many years, he has no idea what to do next. Fear seizes his chest, making it hard for him to breathe. Where has this panic come from? The left side of his body begins to feel numb. From his lips, more as an expletive than a prayer, he mutters, "Dear God . . . dear God . . ."

As suddenly as it had come, the pain eases. Potter looks up from his desk and sees a stranger in the room with him. The stranger says, "Hello, Henry. I'm your guardian angel, Ashby Webb Collins III, Angel Second Class, Yale, 1823. I'm here to help."

"How can I have a guardian angel? I haven't set foot in a church since I was ten years old."

"Oh, that matters not a whit. I represent the Prosperity Gospel division of heaven, and to us, your worldly wealth is a sign that you are one of God's chosen. Why are you then so distressed?"

Potter stammers, "This money has landed in my lap. I . . . I don't know what to do with it."

The angel thought a second and said, "Are you saying you wish this money had never come to you?"

Potter says, "What? Are you out of your cotton-picking mind? Of course not! I just don't know what to do with it."

Angel Second Class Ashby Webb Collins III thinks for a moment and makes a decision: to show Potter how truly he has been blessed, he would show him what life would be like had he never been born. It is a frightening journey for Potter. Scenes he vividly recognizes from his childhood and youth are played out, but he is not in them. In none of the scenes is he there to cheat his playmates, show them the value of hard work and avarice, double-cross his business partners, and bankrupt his father's firms for his own gain.

In fact, his absence has an effect on the entire town of Bedford Falls. Without his guidance, economic growth in the area stagnates. The downtown retail strip remains active, if quaint, but the town is such a backwater that no big-box retailer or national chain can be bothered with it. There's no economic development, no casinos, no growth of any kind. Without Henry Potter's existence, life in Bedford Falls goes on as it always has, a slow, inexorable march toward being a ghost town.

Potter can take it only so long. "Collins! Collins!" he cries. "That's enough! I want my life back! I want to live!"

Instantly, Potter is back at his desk in his office, staring at the money splayed across his desk. Realizing just why this money has been given to him, and the blessed second chance he has received, he makes a vow not to let indecision vex him again. He takes the money and puts it in an offshore bank. As for the Baileys, Potter gets on the phone and calls a senator who is in his pocket. An investigation follows, the Bailey Building & Loan is declared bankrupt, and the officers of the firm are thrown in jail. Potter then puts more pressure on the state politicians to tighten regulations on building and loans, effectively shutting down that industry while allowing established banks to thrive. After a series of fundraisers for pro-business candidates, he is named secretary of the treasury and works hard to ensure that the financial industry can grow robustly without being strangled by pesky regulations and oversight.

And every Christmas, for he isn't unsentimental, he thinks back to his guardian angel, Ashby Webb Collins III. He pours a glass of claret, looks at himself in the mirror, and toasts: "Here's to Henry Potter, the richest man in town."

FORREST GUMP

(1994)

BLUE STATE

    One time, Captain Dan and I was out in the gulf, fishin' for shrimp like we always did, when we see something off in the distance. It's yellow, and it's floating, so we figure we need to go find out what it is. Maybe it was a weather balloon, or else it might have been a boat full of Cuban people, tryin' to escape from their island, like they often did in them days.

But it wasn't a weather balloon nor a raft full of Cuban people. What it was, was an emergency life raft. And in that emergency life raft was a young feller in an Air National Guard flight suit. He looked a little burned up around the edges but he was happy and all. Captain Dan and I sailed the boat over, of course, and helped him in his predicament. Momma always said, whenever you can, to be a good Samaritan.

We lowered the bosun's chair, which is like a little swing from a swing set on the playground, and the man climbed aboard. But for being in his dire predicament, he surely was in a good mood. He was laughin' to himself and tellin' jokes like he was at some fund-raiser for the Rotary Club. I thought for a moment that maybe he was even crazy.

When he finally got on board, I introduced myself. "My name's Forrest. Forrest Gump. And this here's Captain Dan."

"Well, it's awfully decent of you fellas to come pull me out of the drink. Awfully decent."

"What's your name?" I asked.

The man laughed. "Let's not get into that at the moment." He had a twinkle in his eye, and you couldn't help but like him. "So, you're Forrest Gump. Howyadoin', Gumpy? Glad to know ya." He looked at Captain Dan, who did not have a friendly smile on his face. "Gumpy and Stumpy. This is quite the rescue crew. Heh heh. Say, got any liquor on board here? Today has not been one to write home about, believe me."

"No, I'm sorry," I said. "My momma told me to never touch alcohol. And Captain Dan here has been clean and sober for almost a year now, ain't you, Captain Dan?"

"That's right, Forrest," he said, taking the tiparillo cigar out of his mouth, which wasn't lit anyway. "And you better watch your mouth, pal. I don't joke about my legs."

"It wasn't meant as a joke, friend," said the man. "I'm just . . . I'm a nickname guy. You know? It creates a little bonhomie. Y'know, back in my fraternity days . . ."

"You mind telling us what you're doing out here in a life raft?" Captain Dan interrupted.

"Did you fellows happen to see that National Guard jet that came crashing into the water a few hours ago?"

"No, sir," I said.

"Well, me neither," he said. "I was just out doing some fishing. You sure you don't have a little drinkie onboard this tub? Just a beer would do the trick. Or maybe something stronger? Something . . . 'down South America way'?"

"You often go fishing in a flight suit, and without a pole?" asked Captain Dan, who had a suspicious look on his face.

The man laughed. "That must look kinda stupid, huh?"

I told him, "Momma says, stupid is as stupid does."

"Does she now?" he said. "Say, you seem like a couple of nice guys. Why don't you just take me back to port on the QT and not mention this to anyone, and I'll show you both a nice time there. My credit's good anywhere, and this will give me a chance to show you how much I appreciate your saving me.

"And you, young fella, I really do like to hear you talk. Maybe you can tell me a little bit more about your momma, and I can tell you about mine."

And so that's how we ended up with this man, who never did tell us his name or what National Guard unit he was with. But we had a swell time back on shore, if you don't count the stolen police car and the dead prostitute. And it's a shame that the man at the gas station got shot in the kneecap, but he shouldn't have startled our friend like that. It was three days before I found Captain Dan again, and he was real quiet and a little ashamed for a long time after. And he never did want to talk about it again, he told me.

And then, one day a long time later, I read that this fella done got himself appointed president of the United States, on account of his dad and friends and all, but some big men in suits came to visit me one time, to talk about that fun weekend we all had, and said some very scary things to me, even though I'm a decorated veteran. So that's all I've got to say about that.

SPARTACUS

(1960)

RED STATE

The army of slaves, now prisoners of war, sit on a rocky slope awaiting their fate. The Roman soldiers tell them they can avoid the agony of crucifixion if they hand over their leader, the slave called Spartacus.

Hidden in the crowd, Spartacus stares ahead. He knows that revealing his role in the slave rebellion will mean slow, agonizing death, but the alternative will cause innocent men to die. He steels himself to live by his conscience, and rises to declare his identity.

Before he can open his mouth, the slave next to him stands. There's a moment of tense silence between them. Then in a clear voice, the slave announces, "*He* is Spartacus!"

Another stands to add, "And we've got the phone logs to prove it!"

THE ROAD TO BAGHDAD
(1942)

The scene is a crowded Middle Eastern marketplace in a narrow street. At one end a disturbance begins, and through the crowd we see Bob Hope and Bing Crosby running at a fast clip. They wear baggy silk pants and comically big turbans teetering on their heads. Only steps behind them are hairy, muscular palace guards, waving large scimitars, intent on slaughtering the infidels.

CROSBY:
If we ever get out of this alive, remind me to murder you.

HOPE:
Don't worry, pal o' mine, the feeling is mutual.

CROSBY:
Well, don't do yourself in before I get my chance. I called dibs.

HOPE:

I should never have let you talk me into this.

CROSBY:

Me talk you into it? It was *your* idea to come here in the first place. "Travel to Baghdad," you said. "See the world, topple a dictator, spread democracy. . . ."

HOPE:

I didn't want to spread democracy. I only wanted to spread a little wealth, in my direction preferably.

CROSBY:

Well, I hope you're happy now.

HOPE:

Happy? I'm as ecstatic as any man could be at the pointy end of a scimitar.

They dive into a vendor's stall where silks, scarves, and fabrics are sold. The angry guards lumber down the street and pass them by. In a hilariously short period of time, Hope and Crosby emerge from the booth wearing dancing-girl outfits. They proceed carefully down the street, feeling conspicuous.

HOPE:

Think we gave 'em the slip?

CROSBY:

I couldn't find a slip, but I found a nice girdle.

HOPE:

And while we're on the subject of who's to blame here, you were as gung ho about this whole thing as I was. You were supposed to do a little research on the kinds of people living in this sandbox, remember?

CROSBY:

Hey, how did I know it was going to be so easy to tick off the Sunnis?

HOPE:

Well, the Sunni we get out of here, the better.

CROSBY:

Not to mention the Kurds and their ways.

HOPE:

Kurds and ways? Who are we fighting here, Little Miss Muffett?

CROSBY:

It never o-Kurd to me. And man, with those Shiites. . . .

HOPE:

Yeah, we're up to our necks in . . .

CROSBY:

Watch it! We're in enough trouble with the censors.

HOPE:

Poor overworked censors. They're working hard enough on this war as it is. So many pictures of caskets to keep a lid on.

CROSBY:

Remember the old saw, "The first casualty of war is the truth."

HOPE:

Really? Let's not be the second. Duck in here.

They come to a large doorway and push themselves through. On the other side is a small courtyard in front of a mosque, where old men in flowing robes amuse themselves by kicking around a soccer ball.

HOPE:

(*Whispering*) Whoa, partner, wrong door. Back up quietly, we don't want to disturb them.

CROSBY:

What do you mean? Who are these guys?

HOPE:

They're an important group we need to keep on our side.

CROSBY:

What?

HOPE:

Now don't tell me you haven't heard of . . . soccer imams.

They ease themselves back into the street.

CROSBY:

And I suppose you're going to say it was my idea to disband the army.

HOPE:

I never said that. I just thought a five-year weekend pass was too much.

The growls of the guards can be heard again, so our heroes slip into the nearest doorway. After passing through a few closed doors, they find themselves inside a comfortable room filled with pillows, curtains, and assorted luxuries, as well as dozens of beautiful women. Somehow they've stumbled onto the prince's harem. A few of the women gasp, completely unfooled by the costumes the men are wearing.

CROSBY:

Pardon the intrusion, ladies, we're on the lam.

HOPE:

I'd rather have a pork chop, but halal forbids it.

CROSBY:

Say, buddy, do you think there are any WMDs in here?

HOPE:

(*Leering*) You bet your madrassa. Just look around.

CROSBY:

(*Incredulously*) WMDs?

HOPE:

Sure: Wildly Mesmerizing Dames! Women with Massive
Décolletage! Wowie Mamas by the Dozen!

CROSBY:

Hold on a minute, Sheik of Araby. We gotta get out of here.
As tempting as these beauties are, if we don't skedaddle,
we're gonna be in a quagmire.

HOPE:

You'll be in a quagmire, pal. I plan to be in something else.

The women start to get all flirty with both men.

CROSBY:

Well, maybe there's no real rush to get out of here, after all.

HOPE:

See, now you're talking sense. If we cut and run too early, we'd be inviting complete anarchy. Be patient. We cool our heels a while here, then when they're not looking, we head off to . . .

The palace guards burst into the room, swords brandished. The only one who sees them is Crosby.

CROSBY:

Iran!

HOPE:

You've got your tenses mixed up there, amigo. It's "I run, you run, she runs . . ." (*He finally notices the guards.*) *Then*, Iran!

They bombard the guards with large pillows, which get stuck on the points of the swords. Then, Hope and Crosby escape again through a side door.

THE BEVERLY HILLBILLIES

(1993)

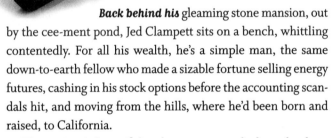

RED AND BLUE STATE

Back behind his gleaming stone mansion, out by the cee-ment pond, Jed Clampett sits on a bench, whittling contentedly. For all his wealth, he's a simple man, the same down-to-earth fellow who made a sizable fortune selling energy futures, cashing in his stock options before the accounting scandals hit, and moving from the hills, where he'd been born and raised, to California.

The setting is beautiful and sumptuous, a lush garden kept tidy by a small army of Mexican laborers, with a pool and marble fountains bubbling soothingly. The opulence and beauty that surround him do not distract Jed Clampett. He's used to having beautiful women around the backyard. After all, who would begrudge a wealthy man's enjoyment of his leisure? Even the additional bathing beauties that came along with Jethro from his televangelism crusade don't distract Jed from his whittling. But he is having a difficult time not getting irritated by his nephew's incessant whining.

"Aww, please, Uncle Jed," Jethro pleads. "You just gotta float me another loan. The note's due on the broadcastin' center, and if the bank takes control of that, I'll lose everything."

Jed says patiently, "Now, Jethro. I already lent ya a heap of money—for the broadcastin' center, the worship center, the conference complex, the amusement park, the Christian cruise line . . ."

"And I'll pay all that back, scout's honor."

"Don't know what in the world a 'Christian cruise line' is supposed to be, anyway."

"I told ya, we got that all figured out. The Caribbean is full of little places we can visit—St. Thomas, St. Kitts, St. Loo-cee-a—"

"God-fearin' people won't go there just 'cuz of the names, boy."

"And we'll restrict dancin' and drinkin' and gamblin' to only one deck . . ."

"This time, I'm gonna have to say no, boy."

"But Uncle Jed—we're havin' a national revival meetin' next week, and I can fer sure pay you back after that."

"How many reservations for the revival you got now?"

"Mmmm. 'Bout twelve."

"How many comped?"

Jethro reluctantly admits, "'Bout ten."

Jed shows his frustration by pursing his lips and squinting. Then he asks his nephew, "You told me you got into this televangelism to spread the good word, didn't ya?"

"Yessir, Uncle Jed. I'm practically finished with the Book of Matthew now."

"Preachin'?"

"Naw, readin'. Despite my genius IQ, you know I'm still a slow reader."

Jed eyes his nephew. "Tell the truth now. You only got into this business so you could meet girls."

Jethro blushes and grins. "Heck, Uncle Jed. You know how it is when a body feels the spirit—suddenly you gots to feel all sorts of other parts, too."

"That ain't what people mean by 'layin' on of hands,' boy," Jed says. "I'm tired of payin' the hush money for these women you been 'feelin' the spirit' with. And Granny can't afford no more bad publicity."

"Doggone it! You always take Granny's side on things. It ain't my fault she's so dumb that she thought she was runnin' for Possum Queen and gets herself elected governor of California."

"Who are you callin' dumb?" shrieks a little voice from behind a hedge, and Granny Clampett busts out with fire in her eyes. "You philanderin', smooth-talkin', blasphemin', collection-plate-stealin' Elmer Gantry!" She starts chasing Jethro around the cee-ment pond with a switch, while the bathing beauties nearby scream in surprise.

"Ow! Ow! Stop it, Granny!"

"And where do you come off on Sundays, callin' me a mass murderer?"

"I din't wanna do it, but you went and approved funds for stem-cell research, and you know my flock's gotta git an answer to that. Why'd you do it?"

"That science holds a lot of promise, boy," Granny says. "And when you get to be my age, you need all the help you can git.

Besides, I gotta do right by all the people of California—that's what they expect from their Possum Queen. As I told 'em many a time, 'From the beaches of Saaaaan Diegooooo, to the mighty redwoods of Humboldt Counteeeee. . . .'"

Jed picks Granny up bodily and sets her down in a chair. "Now, Granny, don't fall into your stump speech agin. . . ."

Jethro says, "Speakin' of redwoods, where's Elly Mae?"

Jed answers, "She took all our tow chains and headed up the coast."

"That dumb ol' girl. She's just going to chain herself to the trees again."

Granny blows her top. "That's another young'un who's ruinin' my good name. And you jus' let her go, didn't ya, Jed? You've grown soft out here."

"Way I look at it," Jed says, "if she's just chained to a tree, I don't have to worry about her blowin' up no power plants. Makes me think we made a mistake to comin' out here to California. Used to be, Saturday night in Bugtussle was all the excitement we needed. Now look at us. We should just pack up and head back to the hills, buy a county or two, and get back to simple livin'."

Granny pulls her hankie out of her apron and sniffles. "I try'n do right by folks—bein' Possum Queen ain't all about kissin' babies and ridin' in parades—but you young'uns do nothin' but humiliate me."

Jethro defends himself. "Well, we wasn't the ones who ran into the state senate last week wavin' a shotgun and shoutin', 'The South shall rise agin!'"

"I was talkin' about South Central LA, you chowderhead!" Granny takes a swing at Jethro and by mistake knocks off the hat, wig, and glasses of one of the groundskeepers. The person they assumed was a Mexican gardener is actually a middle-aged man with gray hair.

The Clampetts all gasp. "Mr. Drysdale!"

To his feet rises the president of the Commerce Bank of Beverly Hills. "Yes, it is I," he admits.

"What're you doin', skulkin' around in the garden and spyin' on honest folks?" Granny asks suspiciously.

"Forgive me . . . I just . . . I couldn't . . .," he stutters, then reaches down and pulls up the gardener squatting next to him. "*She* put me up to it."

Jed reaches over to remove the hat, glasses, and floppy mustache off the second gardener. "Miss Jane!" they all exclaim.

"Greetings all," Jane laughs nervously.

"You mind tellin' me what's goin' on?" Jed says slowly.

"We were undercover," Mr. Drysdale says fawningly. "We wanted to make certain that you weren't hiring any illegals. If the papers ever got hold of that, Granny's political career would be finished."

Jed eyes him suspiciously, aware he's being lied to. Miss Jane steps up and says, "The truth is, Mr. Drysdale didn't want to let you out of his sight. He has been working hard to make sure you and your family won't move back to the hills."

"It's true," the banker admits. "So I need to ask you, what would you think of someplace with bright white beaches, warm ocean breezes, tropical gardens all around . . . ?"

"Weeeeeeell doggies," Jed contemplates, "that sounds right nice."

"Good, then it's settled. We're all headed to the Cayman Islands this afternoon. I've got a plane chartered and all fueled up at John Wayne Airport, waiting for us."

"Cayman Islands?"

Suddenly from behind the hedges surrounding the patio jump up men with walkie-talkies and pistols. "FBI! Don't anybody move!"

The Clampetts all look at each other. As head of the household, Jed announces, "Cayman Islands it is!" as the five of them make a break for the Hummer in the driveway.

CITIZEN CHENEY

(1941)

RED STATE

The noise of the printing presses fills the room, as men decide what tomorrow's headline for *The New York Inquirer* will be. Pressmen gather round a table with Mr. Bernstein, business manager of the paper.

"From what I can tell," says Mr. Bernstein, "I'm afraid we've got no choice." One pressman peels a test sheet off a printing plate. The headline of the *Inquirer* screams:

"VICE PRESIDENT SHOOTS FRIEND IN FACE."

The foreman confirms what he already knows. "This one?" he asks, indicating a second plate, as the test sheet is pulled from it.

"That one," Mr. Bernstein sighs.

"QUAIL, PHEASANTS DECLARED PUBLIC ENEMIES."

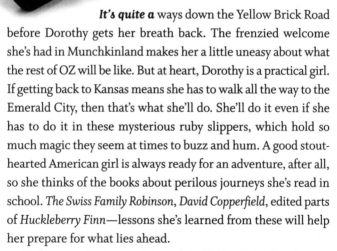

THE WIZARD OF DUBYA

(1939)

PART THREE

RED STATE

It's quite a ways down the Yellow Brick Road before Dorothy gets her breath back. The frenzied welcome she's had in Munchkinland makes her a little uneasy about what the rest of OZ will be like. But at heart, Dorothy is a practical girl. If getting back to Kansas means she has to walk all the way to the Emerald City, then that's what she'll do. She'll do it even if she has to do it in these mysterious ruby slippers, which hold so much magic they seem at times to buzz and hum. A good stout-hearted American girl is always ready for an adventure, after all, so she thinks of the books about perilous journeys she's read in school. *The Swiss Family Robinson*, *David Copperfield*, edited parts of *Huckleberry Finn*—lessons she's learned from these will help her prepare for what lies ahead.

Unfortunately, the condition of the Yellow Brick Road never gets any better. In time it branches off, and there's no sign to indicate the correct way to the Emerald City. While full of pluck and initiative, Dorothy is stumped about which route to take.

A voice says, "Some people like to go that way." Dorothy looks around to see who's speaking, but there's no one around, save for a Scarecrow in tattered, mismatched clothes.

When Dorothy turns her back, the voice speaks again. "Over that way is pretty fabulous, too."

Dorothy turns again but still sees no one. She does notice something strange about the Scarecrow. She stares and asks Toto cautiously, "Wasn't he pointing in the other direction before?"

With a wave of his arms and a swish of his straw, the scarecrow says, "And of course, through no fault of their own, some people like to go *both* ways." With that, the scarecrow lets loose a giggle in spite of himself.

Dorothy's jaw hangs open. Finally, she stutters, "You . . . you can talk!"

"Got it in one, sweetie. The trick is, getting me to shut up."

"What are you doing, sitting up on that pole?"

The Scarecrow shrugs his loosey-goosey arms. "What else would you expect a scarecrow like me to be sitting on?"

"I don't know," says Dorothy. "I'm a stranger in this country. I've seen lots of scarecrows, but I've never heard one talking before."

"Please, have some respect. I'm not a mere scarecrow. I work on the front lines of the OZ security force. This cornfield is just one facet of it. The Heartland Defense Anti-Crow Project was designed to keep these ravenous beasts from endangering all we hold dear in this country."

Dorothy looks at the cornfields all around her. She sees dozens of black birds hopping about and eating the grain. "From here, it doesn't look like it's working too well, if you'll pardon my saying so."

"I'm only referring to what was Phase One of the project," the Scarecrow continues. "In Phase Two, we recalibrated our efforts and rechristened it the Scavenger Blanket Surveillance Initiative."

Dorothy asks, "So, you lowered the goals and changed the name?"

The Scarecrow smiles and nods. "I don't have to tell you what a success it's been. Only . . . only . . . ahhhh . . ."

"You feel like your efforts are scattershot and ineffective?"

"No."

"OZ is still no safer from attacks by crows?"

"No."

"What then?"

"It's hard to concentrate and do my job," said the Scarecrow, "with a pole up my back. You think you can help?"

Apologizing for not helping sooner, Dorothy reaches up to twist the nail holding up the straw man. With a swish and a bump, he lands in a pile on the ground.

"Oh, goodness," Dorothy cries as she runs to help. "Are you hurt?"

"Hurt? You're asking me about hurt? Oh, honey, I know more about hurt than anyone you're gonna meet on this road. And I'm not talking about the pole, heaven knows, although it was no Mardi Gras up there. I'm talking about heartbreak."

"What do you mean?"

"It's so lonely out here, week in, week out. I've got no one to call my special someone."

Dorothy gulps. "Would it help to talk about it?"

The Scarecrow puffs up in rather dramatic fashion. "No," he says, "I'd rather just sing."

If I Only Had a Mate

Gotta say, it gets lonely, to find yourself the only
Talking scarecrow in the state.
But a catcher needs a pitcher, and I'd be forever richer,
If I only had a mate.

We would furnish our apartment, from every store department,
Nothing second-rate.
Choosing sheets, towels, and dishes, we'd fulfill each other's
    wishes,
If I only had a mate.

Oh, I'm the kind of guy
Who needs a spouse by me.
Foot massages and a cup of tea,
And some Oprah on TV.

We'd find a likely pastor, a church of alabaster,
And rush to set the date.
What joy to see us marry, be it Tom, Dick, or Harry,
If I only had a mate.

"Excuse me?" asks Dorothy.

"Hmmmm?" says the Scarecrow, fanning himself from his exertion.

"Harry. You said Harry."

"When?"

"In the song."

"No, I didn't," he laughs, a little too hard. "That wouldn't have made any sense, now would it? 'Harry'! What're you, crazy?"

Dorothy looks at Toto, and they both roll their eyes. Perhaps it's best to say nothing just now. In the uncomfortable silence that follows, Dorothy has an idea. "Say, why don't you come with us to visit the Wizard of Dubya? We're going to ask him to help us find a way back to Kansas."

"*Muy fabuloso!* Maybe he could help me, y'know, find a straw woman."

"From what I hear," says Dorothy, "he's great at setting up straw men."

With that, the two new friends start down the remnants of the Yellow Brick Road, headed for the Emerald City. And Dorothy can't help but notice what a great dancer the Scarecrow is.

After many miles of singing show tunes and dishing about all of OZ's latest celebrities, Dorothy realizes she's hungry. A short distance away, they spot a grove of apple trees full of ripe fruit. Walking closer, Dorothy has a pang of conscience. She feels bad about taking something that isn't hers. The Scarecrow deftly spins it that she's highlighting the gaps in the farmer's security system, and thus doing him a favor.

Dorothy chooses the reddest, ripest apple she can find and

plucks it from the tree. But no sooner has she plucked it than the tree yelps, reaches out its branches, and grabs the apple back. Dorothy and the Scarecrow are shocked. In a gruff voice, the tree says, "What do you think you're doing?"

"We've been walking a long ways," says Dorothy, " and I was hungry, and . . ."

"She was hungry!" the tree scoffs. "And that gives you the right to steal my apples? Why don't you get a job so you can quit leeching? Around here, there's no such thing as a free lunch, *or* a free apple."

"Wait a minute," says Dorothy, "you can talk!"

"And why shouldn't I?" the tree asks haughtily. "In this grove, we're all Cho Sun Vociferous Apple Trees, Patent #23,567,897."

"How . . . How is that possible?"

"If you must know, nosy Parker, delicate bioengineering. By splicing the genes of apple trees, mynah birds, and Venus fly-traps, scientists have created the first talking fruit tree. Now the farmer can be alerted when a tree needs water, when it's attacked by pests, and especially when its apples are being *stolen!*"

"It doesn't seem right, playing God like that," asserts Dorothy. "They allow this kind of thing in OZ?"

"OZ? Hell no!" laughs the tree. "Where you been? OZ stopped scientific research years ago. All these trees came from Korea."

"Heavens to Burpee," mutters the Scarecrow. "Whoever heard of such a thing?"

"Come on, Scarecrow," mocks one of the trees, "you oughta appreciate what it's like, being a fruit . . . tree!" And all the others snicker into their leaves.

This gets the Scarecrow good and steamed. "Why do I get this sass from everyone? I'm just as butch as the next scarecrow," he says, not realizing how his choice of words undercuts his argument.

The trees continue to taunt the Scarecrow and threaten Dorothy with charges of trespassing, theft, and malicious mischief. They even call for security backup from the Cho Sun Midnight Creeper Watchdog Attack Vines, but the vines are malfunctioning and running amok in villages and hamlets to the south. Amid all the noise and shouting, little Toto breaks it up by doing what dogs normally do, all over the roots of the noisiest tree.

"Hey, stop that! You're wrecking my pH balance!" the tree shouts. He and the other trees begin hurling apples at Toto to chase him away. Dorothy and the Scarecrow scoop up the fruit and fill her basket, then retreat to a safe distance. She hungrily bites into the shiniest apple. To her dismay, it tastes like semi-sweetened spackle. Still, it looks just gorgeous.

Something else is marring Dorothy's taste buds: an awful stench of burning oil. As they run from the nasty apple trees, the smell grows stronger and stronger. The Scarecrow doesn't notice it because his nose is only painted on, but Dorothy is so nauseated by the odor that she becomes determined to find its source.

They cross the Yellow Brick Road Repair Zone and enter the woods on the other side. They explore only a short while before they see in a clearing a man made of metal, with thick oily smoke pouring out of the pipe in his head. He is large and powerfully built. He has an ax raised over his head in one hand and a frightening chain saw in the other, but he isn't moving at all.

"My goodness," Dorothy says. "What do you suppose it is?"

"Those apple trees' worst nightmare, I'd say. And wouldn't I *love* to see that happen."

"Don't be catty. We've got to see what this mess is all about."

The two carefully make their way through the ruined landscape, gasping in the smoke and stepping over the tree trunks scattered about. The scene is as ravaged as one can imagine, the opposite of the Scarecrow's tidy green cornfield. Amid all the debris, the metal man stands motionlessly. When they get close enough, they see the Woodsman has a broad face and a strong jaw. He is also biting something that looks like a metal cigar.

"Is it a machine," Dorothy asks, "or is it a person?"

A little squeak comes from the man, which makes them both jump. Dorothy moves closer to hear.

"He said, 'oil can,'" she announces.

"Oil can what?" asks the Scarecrow.

As if in response, the Woodsman starts squeaking at a furious rate. As she jumps back in surprise, Dorothy's foot touches a big can of lubricating oil. She lifts it up and begins squirting the goo on his jaw. Soon it works itself loose, and the metal man finishes the speech he had begun:

". . . and those who tout alternative sources of energy as a solution or a cure-all are living in a dreamworld. It's time to wake up! OZ didn't rise to its place at the front of nations by listening to fanatics. The factories of OZ cannot be powered with windmills and bog bubbles. To repeat, only *oil can* keep OZ growing. Only *oil can* meet our needs, now and in the years to come, if we are simply allowed to search for it. In short, only *oil can* guarantee a bright, secure future for OZ."

"Well, *that* was more than I wanted to know," mutters the Scarecrow.

"If you're a couple of those tree-fondlers," says the man, "then just get the hell out and leave me to rust. Someone else will come by later to save me. You can't stop progress, you forest fascists! Nature Nazis!"

"Please calm down," says Dorothy. "There's no need for name-calling."

"You mean to tell me this guy isn't some kind of eco-freako? Look at him—he's eaten so much whole grain it's coming out his ears."

"It's been a while since I've made it to a salon," the Scarecrow defends himself. "You could use a little polish yourself, ya big homunculus."

"Both of you, stop it!" says Dorothy. While she works at oiling his moving parts, she asks the Woodsman how he came to be in such bad repair. He explains that one day he had been busy at his job managing the forest. He was just about to start clear-cutting his fiftieth acre of the morning when he was "monkey wrenched" by a group of saboteurs. They injected glue in his joints, splattered him with eggs and paint, and put sand in his shorts (which was where his gearbox was). Then they left him there to rust in the field, his chain saw dangling at his side.

"They did a real number on me. My machinery can be fixed, but there's a bigger problem. Before I can go on, there's something else I need. Here, bang on my chest, and you'll find out."

Dorothy knocks on the Woodsman's chest. The sound echoes fiercely.

"A heart?" asks the Scarecrow.

"Yeah, right," the Woodsman snorts. "I'll get right on that. Wait, you're into show tunes, I can tell. Let me crank up the karaoke machine for you. . . ."

IF I ONLY HAD MORE FUEL

In every new McMansion, there lies a growing tension.
This ain't no April Fool.
Do they pay the bills for eating, Grandma's pills, or just the
*   heating?*
If I only had more fuel.

I feel a kind of horror, for my lovely Ford Explorer,
Ironical and cruel.
We're not cruisin' on the byway, no, we're stuck here in the
*   driveway,*
If I only had more fuel.

Oh, we need energy
To run our trucks and cars,
Riding mowers, on-board minibars—
When it's gone here, we'll move to Mars.

Why else would I get mussed up in every little dust-up
From Teheran to Istanbul?
To drill just where I wanna, I could stay in Texarkana.
If I only had more fuel.

As he sings, the Woodsman dances to the edge of the clearing and chops, topples, and uproots huge trees to punctuate his message. His black smoke is everywhere, and the dust stings the eyes of Toto and Dorothy. When he's done, he surveys the littered landscape around him and allows himself a prideful smile.

"To be a steward of the earth," he muses. "It's truly humbling."

Suddenly, Dorothy is struck by an idea. "If you say you need more fuel, why not come with us to visit the Wizard of Dubya? He's going to give the Scarecrow a mate . . ."

"Uh-huh," the Scarecrow says, "a *female* one, I'd like to point out."

"And he's going to send me back home to Kansas."

"That's a kind invitation," says the metal man. "Thanks for your concern."

"Concern?" says Dorothy. "I just figured you could clear us a more direct path through this wilderness."

"Let's take my truck then," offers the Woodsman. "I think I left it over there, someplace." He unclips a key ring from his belt and squeezes the fob, setting the truck's horn honking and its lights flashing.

"Wait a minute," the Scarecrow says. "I thought you were out of fuel."

"What, you've never heard of strategic reserves? Come on, let's roll."

And they all walk over and climb into the Woodsman's new Behemoth XLC. With its V8, 5.6 cubic liter capacity, and 350 horsepower engine, it handles the rough stuff on the Yellow Brick Road like a dream. The Woodsman is obviously proud of his truck; they even share many of the same magnetic yellow ribbons. With the horizon beckoning and the open road ready, they tear off outta there.

The Behemoth XLC cruises over the OZian countryside, tearing up the green turf and making short work of the trip to the Emerald City. With the windows down and Toby Keith blaring out of the speakers, the Woodsman is having the time of his life, although the rough ride's making Dorothy and Toto a bit carsick.

The truck is cruising along at a good clip when from behind a hillock jumps a large gray animal. The Woodsman screams but cannot swerve out of the way. Dorothy and the Scarecrow cover their eyes. There's a loud thump, and the poor animal is thrown up on the hood and all the way over the roof of the Behemoth.

The Woodsman slams on his brakes, and everyone piles out of the truck to see what's happened. On the ground lies a twisted, tangled pile of gray fur. It's so shapeless, no one can even tell what kind of animal it is. They all assume the worst until the pile begins to groan and lift itself to its feet. Eventually, the battered figure can be recognized as a donkey.

"Goodness me," says Dorothy, "are you all right?"

The Donkey gulps and says, "I'm sorry, I'm sorry, I'm sorry . . ."

"What do you have to be sorry for?" asks Dorothy. "We're the ones who hit you."

"Hey," says the Woodsman, "ix-nay on the iability-lay."

"I'm sorry I got in the way," apologizes the Donkey. "I know I must have been a tempting target. It was practically entrapment, what I did . . . what I did just then."

The Woodsman is about to agree with him and complain

about the damage to his paint job, when Dorothy stops him with an upraised hand. "We just want to make sure you're all right," she says. "That was a terrible spill you took. Golly, I'm surprised every bone in your body isn't broken."

"Sorry to disappoint you," says the Donkey sheepishly. "You see, that's part of my problem. My bones have become so rubbery that I can be twisted up like a piece of taffy. For years, I've tried so hard to please everybody. Now, there's nothing solid in me at all."

"You mean, you won't take a stand on anything?" asks the Scarecrow.

"Only if it doesn't offend anyone. Is that all right?"

"Boy, you *are* wishy-washy," Dorothy says. "It's strange. All the donkeys we had on our farm were such stubborn cusses."

"A farm?" exclaims the Donkey. "Oh, I haven't been on a farm in ages. Can't stand the places. They feel so . . . rural. Brrr-rrr-rrr."

"A hard day's work might do you good," says the Woodsman.

The Donkey twists his whole head around to face him, reminding Dorothy of a long-necked goose. "Pardon me, but I know all there is to know about work. Union rules, overtime restrictions, paid vacations, minimum crew of five to fill a pothole. Don't tell *me* about work, I know all about it."

"You know something?" barks the Woodsman. "You're what's wrong with OZ today."

"If you say so. Don't hurt me."

"Why don't you stand up to him?" Dorothy says impatiently.

"Oh, I would if I could. But I have a problem that Medicare can't cover."

IF I ONLY HAD A SPINE

Texas chili, jalapeños, brown mustard, and taqueños,
And pickles soaked in brine.
All of these are much stronger, I can't survive too much
    longer.
If I only had a spine.

If you ask me what I'm thinkin', I'll stand there, dumb and
    blinkin',
Then check the New York Times.
To avoid the nitty-gritty, I'll refer it to committee,
If I only had a spine.

Oh I prefer to lie,
And not get in the way,
Water finds its level, so they say.
You say it doesn't? Well, then . . . okay!

To state a clear position is such an imposition.
Forgive me if I whine.
Choose the former or the latter—oh, does it really matter?
If I only had a spine.

Dorothy's heart goes out to the Donkey. "Why, that sounds awful. You sound like you're being pulled in a hundred different directions."

"You poor long-eared ass, you," commiserates the Scarecrow.

The Woodsman will have none of it. "You people make me sick! 'Boo hoo hoo, I don't have a spine.' Well, go out and find one, Mac, or you'll be a doormat all your life. C'mon, tell us—tell us one thing you absolutely believe with all your heart, one thing you'll stand up for."

"Well," the Donkey snivels, trying to compose himself, "I suppose I sorta . . . think we oughta protect the environment, and not plow the whole thing under for parking lots. Maybe."

The Woodsman grinds his jaw from side to side with a loud, unnerving scrape. "You're hopeless. Let's go, guys."

"We can't just leave him here," Dorothy protests.

"She's right. If he's left on his own, he might sink into the ground altogether," says the Scarecrow.

"Would you like to come with us," asks Dorothy, "and ask the Wizard for a spine?"

"Gosh, I'd like nothing more! But let's not be hasty. There must be other sides to this question to consider."

So the group wastes twenty minutes while the Donkey chews over all aspects and angles of the spine-infusion question. He even brings in a survey team and a bunch of focus groups. Eventually the Woodsman loses his patience. He picks up the limp animal, tosses him in the back of the Behemoth like a wet tarpaulin, and climbs back into the driver's seat. Dorothy, the Scarecrow, and Toto barely manage to get back in the cab before the truck drives off through the countryside, terrorizing other animals in the vicinity.

continued on page 97

MIRACLE ON 34TH STREET
(1947)

In a courtroom sealed to outside observers, a thin bearded man is led to a seat at a table in front of a judge. A blindfold is pulled down from his eyes. The only other people in the room are Mr. Mara, a lawyer for the government, plus two guards and an Army stenographer.

The judge begins the proceedings. "Mr. Mara, will you please state the purpose of this hearing?"

"Your honor," begins Mr. Mara, "the government asserts that this man is a danger to the citizens of the United States, that he is part of a worldwide conspiracy to undermine U.S. security, and that he has repeatedly violated U.S. airspace, including the highly restricted zone above the Capitol Mall."

"Why the secret hearing?"

"Holding an open meeting," the federal attorney explains, "would lead to the unveiling of classified information and endangerment of U.S. interests and intelligence assets."

The judge turns to the accused. "For the purposes of this hearing, will you state your name?"

The old man says, "Kris Kringle, your honor."

"And your citizenship?"

The old man chuckles. "Oh, I don't believe in such things," he says with a twinkle in his eye.

Mr. Mara says, "You have renounced your citizenship to pursue your plans for world domination. Do you believe in fomenting widespread global panic for your own ends?"

The old man pauses a second and says, "Err, I have a global perspective, there's no doubt. And if by 'change' you mean a disruption to humanity's business as usual for something better, then yes, I do. In my opinion, everyone spends so much time thinking about themselves that the children get ignored. The things that grown-ups think are so important are . . ."

Mr. Mara continues, "And for those who seem worthy in your eyes, you've appointed yourself judge, jury, and executioner?"

"Oh heavens no!" says the old man. "How dare you say such a thing?"

Mr. Mara approaches the judge. "Your honor, the government would like to submit as evidence this list, which has been attributed to this individual."

"My list!" exclaims Kringle. "How did you get my list?"

"As you can see, it's a list of names, and each name is clearly marked 'Naughty' or 'Nice.' Addresses are included, and there are even notes about the best ways to gain access to these sites. This is clearly a type of 'hit list' used by this man in his organization."

The judge, wishing to avoid a scene, asks the guards to please put the blindfold back in place on the old man. He then asks the attorney, "How did the government come into possession of this list?"

"We cannot reveal that, your honor, without endangering our intelligence assets in the field."

"How long has the accused been in U.S. custody?"

"Four years, your honor."

The old man says, to himself, "Four years? Has it really been that long? How has Christmas survived without me?"

Mr. Mara cannot resist a taunt. "Don't you worry your beard about it. We've managed to get our shopping done in spite of people like you."

"People like me? *I'm* the only Santa Claus!"

To the judge, Mr. Mara explains, "Delusions of invincibility, of grandeur. He's out to save the world from itself."

"'Santa Claus'?" asks the judge.

"An alias. One of many."

The judge eyes the defendant. "He appears to have lost a little weight."

Mr. Mara says, "The defendant has been treated well, your honor. He gets regular meals and a half hour of sunlight and exercise every day, and his accommodations have been inspected by the Red Cross."

"And their findings?"

"Can be interpreted in different ways, your honor."

The judge sighs and asks, "And where is the evidence that this man is a threat to the United States and should remain incarcerated?"

"Evidence?"

"Yes, evidence."

"Surely your honor is aware that with the designation of an enemy combatant, we don't have to . . ."

"Humor me, please. I'm retiring next week."

"Very well, your honor." Mr. Mara motions the guards to bring forward the evidence: huge mailbags filled with hundreds of letters, all addressed to Santa Claus. The guards hoist the bags and spill the contents all over the judge's desk. "Here are the raw data, your honor, which we believe illustrate how widespread this so-called 'Santa network' is. Because of the overwhelming volume of these communications, the government hasn't analyzed all of it yet."

The judge tiredly picks up one letter, opens it, and reads the contents aloud. "'Dear Santa, How are you? I am fine. I've been extra good. I want a baby brother for Christmas. Thanks. Love Katie.'"

Mr. Mara says urgently, "I would caution your honor to refrain from reading the evidence in the presence of the witness. We haven't yet cracked this code or determined the whereabouts of this operative codenamed Katie."

Behind his blindfold, the man with the white beard cries quietly, "Oh Katie, Katie . . ."

The judge says, "And has the government been able to procure any important intelligence from this man through 'alternative interrogation methods'?"

"No, your honor," says Mr. Mara, with a frustration he cannot hide. "In fact the experience has caused the government to lose fourteen of our interrogators to temporary dementia and mental collapse. They have since been assigned to less sensitive duties."

"How unfortunate," grumbles the judge. "May we hear from the defense counsel at this time?"

This incites fits of laughter in everyone except the judge and the old man. "Hahahaha, good one, judge," Mr. Mara says.

The judge takes off his glasses and rubs his eyes. "The law of the United States leaves me no choice but to remand Mr. Kringle into the custody of the Army until such time as he coughs up what the Army wants to hear, or the administration wishes to look tough before an election again. The prisoner may be removed. This hearing is adjourned. I need to wash my hands very badly."

Federal Attorney Mara watches the skinny old man with the beard being taken away. He allows himself a prideful smile, knowing his work on behalf of the citizens of the United States is having an important effect on the country's security. He also thinks back to a time some thirty years earlier, when he had wished for a twelve-gauge shotgun for Christmas and received a box of football cards instead.

SHERLOCK HOLMES AND THE VIRESCENT RETICULE

RED STATE

In the cozy confines of his drawing room, Sherlock Holmes stuffs his pipe with a superior air while explaining his resolution of their latest mystery to his clueless companion, Dr. Watson. "At that moment, I ascertained that Lord Henry was in fact innocent, and Micklethwait the murderer."

Watson, as ever, is impressed. "Astounding, Holmes. Simply astounding. And you deduced it all with your formidable intellect."

"No, Watson, not at all," says Holmes.

"Well," Watson huffs, "how then?"

"By accepting Jesus Christ as my personal savior and giving him control of my life."

"I see," says Watson, suspicious of an ill-conceived joke. "And not by your intellect, then?"

"To rely on intellect over faith?" Holmes scroffs while lighting his pipe. "Ridiculous vanity, and dangerous besides. I'm surprised at you, Watson."

"Dear me," exclaims Watson, confused. Can you tell me, Holmes, why you handed over Micklethwait to the police?"

Holmes draws on his pipe and says solemnly, "Didn't like his looks, I'm afraid."

Watson huffs again, "Bad luck for him, then, eh?"

"Revelation, Watson. Revelation."

A CLOCKWORK ORANGE

(1971)

BLUE STATE

The scene opens in a small auditorium at a medical center. The room is dark, with a few observers scattered in the shadows. Front and center is our hero Alex, being strapped into a restraining chair. A halo of wires and electrodes hovers over his head. A technician is attaching clamps to his eyelids so he will not be able to shut them. In the front of the room is a large movie screen.

In a voiceover Alex speaks, "Where I was taken to, was like no cine I'd been in before. It seemed a bit crazy to me, but I let them get on with what they wanted to get on with. If I was to be a free young malchick in a fortnight's time, I would put up with much in the meantime, my brothers."

One of the doctors asks over an intercom, "Are you ready for your treatment, Alex?"

The movies begin. Again, we hear Alex in voiceover: "So far the first film was a very good professional piece of cine. A bunch of old-fashioned malchicks were headed after each other in a battle, with old-time weapons and bayonets. They were going at it real horrorshow, but for all the shooting and stabbing, there was nary a drop of red, red krovvy to be viddied. The film began explaining how something called the American Civil War got started. I was able to ignore the schoolbook part and concentrate to the old ultra-violence, but as it droned on, I began to feel real uncomfortable-like. I tried to forget this, concentrating on the next film."

In the shadows of the room, the professionals take notes and whisper to each other. One says in a low voice, "Soon the treatment will begin to take effect."

Alex continues to watch the next film, as the attendant next to him applies tears from a dropper into his strained eyes. His voiceover continues, "The next film showed a young devotchka in an evening gown, being whirled around and around by a tall muscular malchick. They weren't the only ones going at it, as the screen soon filled with a good half-dozen lewdies dancing all in unison, to these tedious Strauss waltzes with lots of violins. They all wore numbers on their backs, and were dancing so synchronized-like that you'd swear they were robots. Why they were showing this to me I knew not, but before very long the sick feeling again rose up in me guts.

"I told the doctors that I needed to be sick, but they ignored my plea, saying it was all part of my cure. And so I suffered through the rest of the entertainment. Cooking shows. Science shows. A show about quilting. A purple dinosaur that kept singing that he loved me. A man in a cardigan sweater who talked so slow that I thought he must have had a stroke or some such thing. Soon after this torture, I sort of blacked out."

These treatments continue for several sessions, all of which Alex endures, for this experiment is his ticket out of the penitentiary. In two weeks, Alex is unveiled to a meeting of scientists and doctors. His conversion is hailed as a success by those in charge. Alex stands proudly before them in his Dockers and L.L. Bean sweater, happy to be escaping confinement and strangely craving a tall skim latté half caf, half synthemesc.

Alex is released again to fend for himself in society. It isn't long, however, before the incidents begin and the limits of his "reeducation" become clear. A week after Alex's release, neighbors throw a barbecue to salute his freedom, but when they serve pork chops with red Chablis from a box, Alex collapses, retching and insisting on bottled water. When his friends playfully kidnap him and take him to a NASCAR rally, Alex causes a scene by loudly describing a *Frontline* episode about big oil companies.

But the final straw comes when Alex volunteers to work the pledge drive phone banks during a *Monty Python's Flying Circus* marathon, and five callers in a row try to get him to do the "Wink Wink, Nudge Nudge" routine. The resulting carnage, which the press later dubs "The Tote Bag Massacre," is broadcast for the world to see. In the end, the researchers' plan to create a population of informed, rational citizens via television proves a terrible failure, and Alex gets a development deal for reality shows with Spike TV.

THE WIZARD OF DUBYA

(1939)

PART FOUR

After the Behemoth XLC crashes through the last stretch of forest, the four friends look out over an expansive plain. The sky is a wondrous blue with a few puffy clouds, and in the distance are the spires of a magnificent city.

"Do you see it?" the Scarecrow asks in excitement. "Do you see it?"

"The Emerald City," the Woodsman marvels.

Dorothy is puzzled, however. "For an emerald city, it doesn't look very green."

"Probably just a trick of the light," says the Woodsman. "Haze and particulates and such. Our target's in sight—let's roll!"

With his iron cigar chomped tightly between his teeth, the Woodsman pushes his metal to the pedal to the metal. Soon the Behemoth is cruising down the Yellow Brick Road again. Dorothy notices that, as they get closer to the capital city, the condition of the Yellow Brick Road gets better and better—much better than it was out in the boondocks in Munchkinland. Just a coincidence, she tells herself.

The four adventurers and Toto are happy and excited as they approach the Emerald City. When they can drive no closer, they park their truck and walk up to the first checkpoint. They patiently wait while disinterested guards in official uniforms herd them through metal detectors, inspect Dorothy's basket, and confiscate their shoes. At the second, third, and fourth checkpoints, they still keep their spirits up. But by the fifteenth checkpoint, their patience is wearing thin (although the Scarecrow is having an inordinate amount of fun with the cavity searches). Considering what they've been through and how tantalizingly close they are to their goal, the Woodsman can be forgiven when he loses his temper around the thirteenth checkpoint and fries out all the circuitry in the X-ray equipment.

"Oh, I'm beginning to think we'll *never* make it into the city," whines the Spineless Donkey, quivering at the sight of the police dogs behind the next fence. "They already think we're troublemakers. They're going to ship us off somewhere where no one will ever hear from us again."

"They can't do that, can they?" Dorothy asks. "Legally?"

"Well, there's legal," the Woodsman says, "and then there's legal."

"Cheer up, old pal," says the Scarecrow. "If we're getting this much attention, there's no doubt the Wizard really will see us. Otherwise, we'd already be disappeared."

"Damn straight," the Woodsman agrees, as he retrieves his ax and buzz saw. "They're only looking for dangerous individuals. What's the Donkey going to do, soften himself over everyone?"

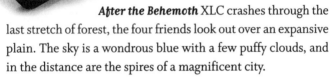

THE WIZARD OF DUBYA

(1939)

PART FOUR

RED STATE

After the Behemoth XLC crashes through the last stretch of forest, the four friends look out over an expansive plain. The sky is a wondrous blue with a few puffy clouds, and in the distance are the spires of a magnificent city.

"Do you see it?" the Scarecrow asks in excitement. "Do you see it?"

"The Emerald City," the Woodsman marvels.

Dorothy is puzzled, however. "For an emerald city, it doesn't look very green."

"Probably just a trick of the light," says the Woodsman. "Haze and particulates and such. Our target's in sight—let's roll!"

With his iron cigar chomped tightly between his teeth, the Woodsman pushes his metal to the pedal to the metal. Soon the Behemoth is cruising down the Yellow Brick Road again. Dorothy notices that, as they get closer to the capital city, the condition of the Yellow Brick Road gets better and better—much better than it was out in the boondocks in Munchkinland. Just a coincidence, she tells herself.

The four adventurers and Toto are happy and excited as they approach the Emerald City. When they can drive no closer, they park their truck and walk up to the first checkpoint. They patiently wait while disinterested guards in official uniforms herd them through metal detectors, inspect Dorothy's basket, and confiscate their shoes. At the second, third, and fourth checkpoints, they still keep their spirits up. But by the fifteenth checkpoint, their patience is wearing thin (although the Scarecrow is having an inordinate amount of fun with the cavity searches). Considering what they've been through and how tantalizingly close they are to their goal, the Woodsman can be forgiven when he loses his temper around the thirteenth checkpoint and fries out all the circuitry in the X-ray equipment.

"Oh, I'm beginning to think we'll *never* make it into the city," whines the Spineless Donkey, quivering at the sight of the police dogs behind the next fence. "They already think we're troublemakers. They're going to ship us off somewhere where no one will ever hear from us again."

"They can't do that, can they?" Dorothy asks. "Legally?"

"Well, there's legal," the Woodsman says, "and then there's legal."

"Cheer up, old pal," says the Scarecrow. "If we're getting this much attention, there's no doubt the Wizard really will see us. Otherwise, we'd already be disappeared."

"Damn straight," the Woodsman agrees, as he retrieves his ax and buzz saw. "They're only looking for dangerous individuals. What's the Donkey going to do, soften himself over everyone?"

After the last checkpoint, Dorothy and the others stand outside the walls of the great city. All is quiet except for the wind blowing some litter around. The main door to OZ is large and foreboding, but Dorothy tries not to be afraid. She walks up the front steps and pushes the doorbell.

Oh, the deafening sound that follows! Bells, sirens, gongs, klaxons, buzzers, and steam whistles all erupt with an earsplitting clamor. Dorothy and her friends cover their ears in pain until the sound dies down. Then a small panel in the middle of the door opens and a strange man with a mustache sticks his head through.

"Who rang that bell?" the man screeches. "Can't you read the sign?"

"What sign?" asks the Scarecrow.

"The sign on the . . . on the . . . oh rats, someone's stolen it again." The man withdraws from the window a moment, then emerges with another sign. He hangs this one up and disappears again. Dorothy reads the sign out loud to the others:

We appreciate your patience
while we install systems that will make
the Emerald City more secure.
Please use the Manual Guest Announcement Indicator
in the meantime.
DEPART. OF SECURITY OVERSIGHT,
IN PARTNERSHIP WITH THE JONES-STENKINS CORP.
The Wizard

Following instructions, Dorothy grabs the huge knocker on the door and lets it swing with a loud thud. The strange man sticks his head out of the panel and says, "Well, that's more like it. State your business."

In one loud voice they announce, "We want to see the Wizard!"

"Oh, so you want to see the Wizard, eh? Won't happen, you're a security risk."

"A security risk?" asks the Scarecrow. "Why?"

"There are fifteen checkpoints leading up to this door," he explains, "and you got stopped at every one."

"So?"

"So, the checkpoints are there to identify security risks. If you were detained at each one, you must be a problem."

"We had no choice," the Donkey says.

The doorman puts up his hands. "If you had nothing to hide, then you'd have nothing to worry about."

"But you people set up the checkpoints," the Scarecrow says.

"Exactly," smiles the doorman. "To weed out security risks. Looks like they've done a good job. Now, be off with you."

"No, we need to see the Wizard," the Woodsman says. "We were sent by the Witch of the North."

This gives the doorman pause. "Prove it."

"Dorothy's wearing the ruby slippers that she gave her," the Scarecrow says.

The doorman is greatly impressed by this and closes his little panel. Within half a minute, he opens the huge door and welcomes them in. After surrendering their credentials and submitting to an ocular scan and DNA samples, they are admitted to the Emerald City.

Oh my, but it is a busy place! People walking briskly along, carriages and town cars whizzing by, talking heads on televisions everywhere, vendors selling T-shirts and souvenir spoons to tourists from Boboland. There are stately buildings, monuments, statues, and plazas, some of which are even open to the public. One odd thing Dorothy notices about the Emerald City, though, is the complete lack of emerald. There's no green to be seen anywhere, nor red or yellow or purple or any color at all. In fact, there are hardly any shades of gray. If any place could ever be called the Black & White City, this is it.

They turn back and ask the doorman if they are in the right place, but he can't understand what they are talking about. Everything looks fine to him. "Many people like to put these on," he says, holding out a box full of rose-colored glasses. "These can be locked around one's head for the length of one's visit and give a very enjoyable simulation of color in high-def, with weather updates, sports scores, and a stock-market crawl at the bottom."

Too much information, the four friends agree. They turn down his offer and walk ahead into the city.

It has been such a long journey, and the Black & White City is obviously such a very important place, that the four friends decide they need to freshen up before going to see the Wizard. Dorothy finds a spa where she can get a facial, oil massage, and hot rock treatment ("When in OZ . . .," she says to herself). The stylist talks her into a more professional-looking hairstyle, but

Dorothy refuses to wear the blue business suit she's offered. Instead, she has the sleeves and hem of her gingham dress shortened again, and puts on a fresh girdle and ACE bandages. The stylists go into swoons about her ruby slippers, so those stay, too. Dorothy enjoys being pampered and fussed over, but she can't understand why the stylists all refer to themselves as "friends of Dorothy" when she's never met any of them before in her life.

The Scarecrow, with no apparent qualms, gets himself stuffed with brand-new hay, then stuffed again, and stuffed again, until it feels just right. Opting for business casual, he gets a new outfit from Dolce & Gabbana, plus some Italian boots and very expensive silky underwear that give him an extra feeling of confidence. He becomes miffed when he hears a salesman mutter a joke about "Queer Eye for the Straw Guy," and insists that his fiancée, "who is a supermodel," will appreciate his new finery.

The Woodsman visits OZ County Choppers and indulges himself, installing a 4-bolt main 454 engine bored .0060 to 482 cubic inches, a 6-speed Tremec transmission, Stage III 950 cfm double pumper Brodix B-1 heads, a Ford 9″ rear end with 4 link suspension, leather seats, chrome mud flaps, a six-DVD changer, XM Radio, and GPS tracking system.

And the Donkey has a flea bath.

Clean and confident, the pilgrims regroup and set off for the palace of the Wizard. The Donkey feels butterflies in his stomach, but he isn't the only one. Many mysterious tales have been told about the Wizard and his power: how he can magically peer into people's hearts and see their true intentions, how he can solve intractable problems seemingly on gut instinct, how his decisions are always the right ones no matter what ends up happening. It's said that once he was nearly defeated by an itty-bitty pretzel, but no one really knows the whole story. The pretzel was undoubtedly enchanted, infused with magic to subdue the Great Dubya, and this mystery only adds to his aura of invulnerability.

Out on the street there's a great commotion among all the inhabitants of the city. People are shouting and running, with fearful looks on their faces. It doesn't take long for Dorothy to figure out what's upsetting them: In the black-and-white cityscape, the bright bars of colored lights that dominate one edge of the plaza nearly blind her. One bar blinks as a siren blares, declaring a warning of some kind. From bottom to top, the array of bars explains:

RED

DANGER. BE ON GUARD.

MORE RED

MORE DANGER. BE JUMPY AND SUSPICIOUS.

MOST RED

DANGER LEVEL INCREASING. BE READY TO JOIN
AGITATED MOBS.

MOSTEST RED

DANGER LEVEL INCREASING TO DANGEROUS LEVELS.
AVOID MAKING LONG-TERM PLANS OR BUYING GREEN
BANANAS.

SO RED YOU DON'T WANT TO KNOW

ANY INQUIRIES REGARDING THIS LEVEL OF RED WILL
BE PROSECUTED TO THE FULLEST EXTENT OF THE LAW.

Since the "Most Red" sign is flashing, Dorothy and her companions take its advice and join an agitated mob nearby. Frightened voices are jabbering all around:

"What should we do? What's going on?"

"The Wizard will explain it!"

"I like him. He's a reg'lar feller."

"Smart enough not to appear too smart."

"Yeah, I'd sure like to have a beer with him, if, y'know, he ever drank beer."

Within a short time, the mob has wound its way through the city, right to the steps of the Palace of the Wizard. A guard on the palace steps is doing his best to calm everyone down, although he seems a bit flustered himself.

"Don't be alarmed, folks . . ." he starts to say.

A man shouts, "The sign *told* us to be alarmed!"

"Yes, well, be *vigilant*, certainly. Attentive, even. But try and be alarmed in a positive way. Go out and do some shopping, eh? That'll show our enemies, that we can be alarmed yet still carry on with the things that make us great."

"Why won't you tell us what's going on?" asks another man.

"If I knew what was going on, I'd tell you," the guard says. "But . . . but we can't all know what's going on, because then . . . then . . . *everybody* would know. Especially our enemies. Can't have that. To keep them in the dark, we all have to do our part staying in the dark, too. Now everyone, please, go back home. The Wizard has got matters well . . . in hand . . . I hope. Go be alarmed, but only just enough, and do what you normally do. Don't forget your duct tape! Big sale on duct tape at the mall!"

Presented with these and other empty entreaties, the crowd disperses, although reluctantly. Dorothy and her friends come up to the exhausted-looking guard and say, "Please sir, we'd like to see the Wizard of Dubya."

The guard retorts, "Orders are . . . nobody can see the Great Dubya. Not nobody, not nohow."

"Oh, but it's very important," Dorothy insists.

"He's in conference with himself," says the guard, looking around nervously, "on account of this . . . new alarm thing. You can bet he's working on that. This. And even if he wasn't . . . you wouldn't have been able to see him anyway, unless it was a town hall meeting."

"Town hall?" asks the Donkey.

"Yes, but those take months to produce . . . writing, auditions, rehearsals. I don't know when there'll be another one. Probably never. All that spontaneity gets in the way of the Wizard's work."

"You seem to know a lot about how things work around OZ," says the Woodsman.

"No! No! I'm completely out of the loop. Ask my lawyer."

The Woodsman walks up to the guard and tells him confidentially, "We know the Wizard is a busy, busy man. The fate of the whole of OZ rests on his shoulders. We only want to see him so we can tell him of our support for all his policies and what a great job he's doing as leader."

"Oh?" the guard says, a little surprised. "That's what you want to see him about?"

"That's right," says the Woodsman smoothly. "Just to show our support."

As your mother always told you, a good word will get you far, and a good word is exactly how our friends get in to see the Wizard of Dubya. Of course, a good word needs a messenger, so they talk with the guard's brother-in-law, who is a registered lobbyist in the Black & White City, and slip him 200 large. The lobbyist then carries the good word and some money to a friend at a group called the OZ Freedom Progress Society, which carries the word and some money to the OZians for Decency and Niceness (an affiliate of the Perversion Prevention League), which carries the word and some money to the OZ Personal Initiative Initiative, and so on down the line. Our friends wait about an hour, while phone calls are made and e-mails sent, and finally the guard welcomes them into the Palace of the Wizard and shows them to a special waiting area.

"How did you know what to do?" the Scarecrow asks.

"Look at me," the Woodsman says with his metal arms outstretched. "You think I don't know how to grease wheels?"

They are escorted into a waiting room with shiny marble floors, gold axes and shields on the walls, and many prominent, inspiring displays of the OZian flag. This flag has been newly designed, of course, made of fireproof material with the words "Strength Through Might—We're # 1!" printed along the bottom. The atmosphere in the room conveys the majesty of the Wizard's power and the dignity of his position, an impression only slightly tarnished by the presence, smack in the middle of the room, of an elaborate, oversized bronze statue of a Gillykin steer being roped by a manly Munchkin cowboy. The Scarecrow heaps praises on it, but probably for its camp value. Dorothy, an innocent child, thinks it's all very impressive, even more impressive than the poultry and rabbit pavilion at the state fair.

Dorothy and her friends are stuck in the waiting room for quite some time. Eventually, the gilded doors of the room open as if by magic, beckoning them into the next chamber. This massive hall is the biggest room any of them have ever seen. Their footsteps echo unnervingly. Torches blaze in brackets on the walls, and the ceiling is so high it's almost out of view. At the far end of the room is a most terrifying sight: As trombones sound and balls of flame shoot up on either side, the countenance of the mighty Wizard of Dubya hovers over a gilded throne. His gigantic face is resolute and steely, squinting inscrutably. When he opens his mouth to speak, the hall reverberates with his nasal twang.

"Come forward!"

The four companions nearly jump out of their shoes with fright. They try to begin walking forward, but they're shaking too much to move. (The Spineless Donkey looks like he's about to explode.)

"I said, come forward!"

They take small, tentative steps. The flames shoot up again around the floating face, nearly scorching the ears protruding on either side. The voice booms, "I am Dubya, the Great and Powerful! That means . . . I do . . . great and powerful things. Things that need doing . . . in a great and powerful manner. Do I make myself clear?"

Dorothy feels she's been the start of all this, so she bravely steps forward. "If you please, I . . . I am Dorothy . . . the small and meek. We've come to ask . . ."

"Silence!" roars the head.

The startled Dorothy runs back to her friends. "Oh, Jiminy Crickets!"

"The Great and Powerful Dubya knows why you have come! Of course I know why. It's my job to know why. And I will do the job that is mine to do. My job is to do my job."

Dorothy grows a little less frightened as the head continues: "Sometimes I don't get enough credit, you know, for being on top of things, but I am. Nothing gets by us around here. And by us, I mean me. Trust me. Now, regarding your situation. We've been following it with great interest. And we will continue to follow it until the chance . . . because by following, we lead . . . or can lead . . ."

There's an awkward pause, and the Wizard sets off his fire jets. The startling roar has them shaking again.

"Okay, you there, Woodsman. Step forward. Can I call you Rusty? Heh heh."

The Woodsman opens his mouth to speak, but the Wizard goes on. "So, you come to me looking for more fuel? I tell ya, Rusty, that's what's been goin' on ev'rywhere . . . it's what we're concerned with . . . and we are concerned . . . but freedom can't be mortgaged, or held hostage . . . we can't do that, plain and simple . . . just so . . . if . . ."

The flames shoot up again, cutting off the Wizard in mid-sentence and chasing the Woodsman back a few steps.

"And you, Scarecrow?" says the floating head. "Hay there. Heh heh. Hay, how are ya? Heh heh. So, Cow Chow, you've got the effrontage to . . . to . . . to ask me for a mate? Like I'm some kinda matchmaker or somethin'?"

"Oh yes, your honor," fawns the Scarecrow. "I mean, yes, your Excellency. Yes, you handsome hunk of head!"

"I'm all in favor of finding mates . . . mating is the bedrock of our communities, where mating is cheered on . . . back in college, anyway it was, and I can't tell you some of those stories, heh heh. . . ."

Again, the flames erupt, punctuating the Wizard's statement before he could ramble on again.

"Enough!" the Wizard says, while the Scarecrow yelps half in fear and half in excitement. "And you, Donkey! Beast of Burden. Juan Valdez. . . .You want to know what I think of immigration, right, Burrito?"

"I . . . um . . . I . . . Sure, whatever you say."

"Well, now's not the time," says the head. "Can't be blaming the fingers we point. This problem needs solving, not fingers-blaming-pointing. I need you to trust us on this, and let us do the job. You know, back in Gillykin we have a saying: If it walks like a duck, and talks like a duck . . . then . . . you have to . . . y'better duck, is what it means . . ."

The Donkey sinks down and lies motionless on the floor. Dorothy runs up to her friend, then accuses the Wizard, "You ought to be ashamed of yourself. He's fainted, when he came to you for help."

"Wha . . . Huh?" says the Donkey. "I guess I fell asleep."

The flames roar once more, and trombones blare, along with the sound of jet planes and rockets. Security men step out from the shadows and stand at the ready, and the head bellows, "Silence, whippersnapper! I had a dog named Snapper once, you remind me of him. Heh. Anyway, I never said I wouldn't grant your requests. I'm a man of compassion. Every day, compassioning is what I do. I would never deny I wouldn't grant your requests, cuz that's not what people look for in a wizard. But first, you need to do something for me. Not quota pro quota or anything, but when you want help, your help has to be . . . has to come back. You have to trust the help will bounce back. That's the glory of the system here. That's what makes us the envy of the world. Now, here's what you gotta do: Bring me the broomstick of the Wicked Witch of the West."

The four pilgrims look at one another. Dorothy asks, "Who?"

"Let me repeat so you can understand: The Wicked Witch . . . of the West."

"I heard you clearly," Dorothy says, "but it's just that, we've never heard of her. We've heard of Winkies, Growleywogs, the Wicked Witch of the Northeast. . . ."

"We're fighting for freedom on many fronts," intones the Wizard. "We know this witch has a broomstick and won't hesitate to use it."

"To get the broomstick," quivers the Donkey, "won't we have to kill her?"

"The broomstick needs to be brought to justice," says the floating head. "And the witch does too. I will not rest . . . I mean, you will not rest until this is done. After that, all things being suitable in the situation, your requests will be considered in a manner that is timely, as befit them. And me. I."

"Just the four of us?" asked the Scarecrow. "Can't we find some others to bring along?"

"No, no time. This imminent threat is immediate, and it is presently now at hand. The Mighty Dubya has spoken. Good luck to ya. God bless OZ."

Then the Wizard's head waves, turns away, and disappears. More fire blazes, and seems to startle the head some as it exits. The four friends are escorted out of the hall and off the palace grounds, and deposited in the street by the security detail.

continued on page 133

THE GRAPES OF WRATH

(1940)

RED STATE

In the dark campsite, around a meager fire, Ma Joad, matriarch of the proud-yet-battered Okie family, and her son Tom contemplate the future. Tom's killed a man, and he knows that if he stays, the police will cause trouble for his family and the rest of the migrants until he's captured. Tom tells his tearful mother that he needs to strike out on his own.

"How'm I gonna know 'bout you?" she begs. "They might kill you an' I wouldn't know. They might hurt you. How'm I gonna know?"

Tom laughs uneasily. "Well, maybe it's like Casy says, a fella ain't got a soul of his own, but on'y a piece of a big soul—the one big soul that belongs to ever'body—"

"Oh, Tom," she says, "that Casy was a sacrilegious Socialist crackpot who's drownin' in hellfire now. But how will I know about *you*?"

"It don't matter," he reassures her. "I'll be all aroun' in the dark. I'll be ever'where—wherever you look. Wherever there's a fight so people can live without no government innerference in their lives, I'll be there. Wherever there's a fight to make sure everyone's marriage is safe and reg'lar, with no nancy-boy stuff goin' on, I'll be there. An' when our people eat the stuff they raise, an' live in the houses they build, enjoyin' the benefits of a free market subsidized to reflect true American values, why, I'll be there, too."

Ma shakes her head and says slowly, "I don't understan' what you talkin' 'bout, Tom."

Tom rises and says dryly, "Me neither. But if I jus' keep listenin' to the fellas on the talk ray-dio, it should all make sense someday. Gimme your hand, Ma. Good-by."

With that, Tom slips off into the darkness.

CASABLANCA

(1942)

BLUE STATE

On the foggy tarmac of the airport, in this city of refugees fleeing the carnage in war-torn Europe, Rick Blaine explains how things have to be to his old flame, Ilsa. "I've got a job to do, too. Where I'm going, you can't follow. What I've got to do, you can't be any part of. Ilsa, I'm no good at being noble, but it doesn't take much to see that the problems of three little people don't amount to a hill of beans in this crazy world. Someday, you'll understand that."

Ilsa's eyes well up with tears. Rick puts his hand to her chin and raises her face to meet his own. He smiles and says, "Here's looking at you, kid."

As Rick and Renault, the French captain, look on, Ilsa and her husband Victor Laszlo leave to board the plane. They enter a line to pass through the security checkpoint. Even though she and Victor are the only people boarding the plane, getting through security takes more than an hour. First, all their carry-on luggage is inspected for knives, guns, box cutters, matches, lighters,

gels, suspicious liquids, questionable semiliquids, venomous snakes, car batteries, self-inflating rafts, and propane tanks. Next, the security detail heads off for a thirty-minute break. When they return, the metal detector starts to malfunction, so Ilsa and Victor are taken back to the terminal for strip and cavity searches. By the time they get back, the Nazi commander Major Strasser has already arrived, uncovered the plot, and been shot dead by Rick.

As Ilsa and Victor walk up the steps to their waiting plane (in slippers, since their shoes have been confiscated), a French police patrol arrives. Captain Renault informs them, "Major Strasser has been shot." He pauses and looks at Rick long enough for him to get nervous. Then Renault orders his men, "Round up the usual suspects."

The soldiers are taken aback. They're unsure whether Renault is aware of what he's just ordered. After a tense silence, Renault says, "All right, all right, round up *everybody*."

The soldiers speed off in their jeeps. Rick smiles and asks, "Profiling problems, Louie?"

Renault sighs. "Profiling problems, Ricky."

007:
THE SPY
WHO OUTED ME
(1977)

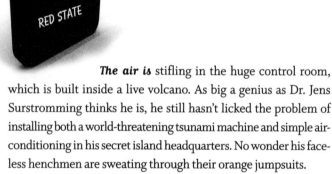

RED STATE

The air is stifling in the huge control room, which is built inside a live volcano. As big a genius as Dr. Jens Surstromming thinks he is, he still hasn't licked the problem of installing both a world-threatening tsunami machine and simple air-conditioning in his secret island headquarters. No wonder his faceless henchmen are sweating through their orange jumpsuits.

But personal comfort is not on the mind of superspy James Bond. The countdown has started over the room's loudspeakers. The leaders of the free world have not met Dr. Surstromming's demands to strip to their underwear, wrestle in Jell-O, and give him the pay-per-view rights. Now he is making good on his threat to unleash tidal waves on the coastal cities of the world. Only Denver, La Paz, and Peshawar will be spared. Bond has to stop him, but presently he is chained hand and foot, suspended over a tank of hungry tiger sharks, and slathered from head to foot in chum. As bits of the bait fall off him and into the water, the hungry sharks thrash impatiently.

Dr. Surstromming strolls up to the side of the tank alongside his slinky paramour, Sumptuous BoomBoom. "And so, Mr. Bond, the world's leaders will soon learn how dangerous it is to ignore monomaniacal madmen."

"What?" Bond asks.

"I said, the world's leaders will . . ."

"I can't hear you!"

Dr. Surstromming takes a remote control out of his pocket and holds down a button. The female voice doing the countdown over the loudspeakers gradually lowers in volume.

"Is that better?" asks the rogue scientist.

"Much."

"As I was saying . . ."

"Jenssy," Sumptuous BoomBoom interrupts, "that countdown is one of my best performances. The CD is being released next week. *Why'd* you turn it down for *him*?"

"Don't worry, my sweet, we can play it again later. Now, Mr. Bond . . ."

The evil genius is stopped in midgloat by a series of explosions that rock the cavernous chamber. True to form, the orange-clad henchmen run helter-skelter across catwalks and helipads. Bond's shackles slip a bit from their moorings. Then down a cable suspended from the ceiling rappels the leather-clad figure of Mrs. Bond, who prefers to operate under her professional name of Natanya. A veteran of many years in the field, she's in fine shape for a woman her age, although the leather jumpsuit is perhaps less than flattering.

"It's about bloody time," says Bond in mock peevishness.

"Don't start with me," his wife says. "Didn't I ask you three weeks ago to check the oil in the van? So what happens to me today? I have a breakdown on the way to the cleaners."

"The van is *your* car," says Bond, still dangling precariously over certain doom. "*You've* got to maintain it."

Natanya lands on the ground and squares off with Sumptuous BoomBoom. "Do you know how long I had to wait for the government to send a tow truck?"

"Honey," her husband cautions, "state secrets, hmmmm?"

In her white evening gown, Sumptuous BoomBoom levels a karate kick at Natanya, who ducks it and tries for a kidney punch. For a moment, Bond and Dr. Surstromming watch the fight, mesmerized, as are a dozen or so nearby henchmen. Natanya tackles BoomBoom into a bank of computer monitors and delicate equipment which are destroyed in a spray of sparks. More explosions shake the hideout, and Bond's chains slip further.

"I'm confused," says Dr. Surstromming. "When I read in the papers that your wife was a spy, I thought it was disinformation. She couldn't really be a spy, I told myself. No one in your government could be so sloppy with secret data that they'd casually mention her status to a hatchet-man columnist."

"You'd be surprised," says Bond, stalling for time.

"But then, I thought, maybe you'd think I'd think that, and that would make her a spy again. But hold the phone! That again was too transparent a gimmick. Surely your government isn't so moronic they would put such a clumsy plan in place and pray it would work."

"But you should've taken it one more step," says Bond. "Ironically, for an monomaniacal genius bent on taking over the world, you didn't overthink enough."

They watch the fight some more, and Dr. Surstromming says, "I gotta admit, she ain't bad for her age."

Natanya barks, "Will you quit talking about me like I'm not here?" Sumptuous BoomBoom knocks her over with a jujitsu flip, then is upended herself.

"Hey, no offense," says the evil doctor. "I just figured you as someone with a desk job."

"Desk job? How's *this* for a desk job?" Natanya picks up a handy table and pins her opponent violently against another control panel. In a shower of electricity and smoke, Sumptuous BoomBoom spastically shakes and screams. Soon sparks fly out of her ears and mouth, and she falls onto the table like a broken marionette. For all her humanlike qualities, it turns out Sumptuous BoomBoom was nothing but a slutty robot.

"Hey, Jenssy," Bond says from above, "can you make one of those for me?"

Panting and exhausted, Natanya picks herself up and says, "You watch it, buddy. You're already on thin ice."

"Come on, I was joking . . ."

"I saw the way you were watching her while we fought."

"Please, please!" says Dr. Surstromming. "If I wanted to hear nagging, I would've programmed it into my bimbo."

With one final kick, Bond pulls the chain around his feet out of the wall and swings it to wrap around Dr. Surstromming's neck. With a quick tug, he pulls the evil genius off his feet and

Surstromming falls backward, into the shark-filled tank. With the extra weight, however, the other chain from which Bond is suspended begins pulling from the rock. As it breaks off, the bait-covered Bond plummets toward the water, only to be lassoed by a tether and pulled out of harm's way by his wife. As the sharks make an enthusiastic lunch out of Dr. Surstromming, and explosions continue to destroy the control room, Natanya unlocks his restraints with a ballpoint pen and some WD-40. "I learned it from Heloise," she says.

Bond looks up at his wife and says sincerely, "Thank you for sending me on this assignment, dear."

She smiles. "Anything to get you out of the house," she says, as they make their escape.

AN INCONVENIENT TRUTH

(PLUS SOME OTHER DOCUMENTARIES)

(2006)

The movie opens with some lovely shots of Patagonia, where the South American mountains are frozen in the clutches of a great ice field. Lonely and forbidding, yet exotic and tantalizing, there's a stark beauty to this windswept glacier that is only fully appreciated from the comfort of your own couch.

Quick cut, to scenes of a flock of penguins marching across a rocky landscape. Are there penguins in Patagonia? That's a stumper. I didn't think there were, but that's why a person watches documentaries, I suppose, to learn stuff. Hell, I didn't even know there was a place *called* Patagonia before this. I bet the company had to pay a pretty penny to have such a big chunk of land named after itself. Maybe they're moving all their factories down there, to test winter weather conditions.

Speaking of winter, it sure looks like it's getting cold for those penguins. They're all huddled around for warmth during a blizzard. The sound of the wind cuts right through me. The poor things! It must be hard to balance an egg on your feet when it's that cold.

Eggs. Yeah, that's a good idea. Another quick cut. Some guy with a horseshoe mustache ordering at McDonald's. Hope it's an Egg McMuffin. Or even a McGriddle. Those things have pancakes with the syrup *baked right in.* Score one for American technology, baby!

Baked. Looks like Patagonia's baking, all right. That whole glacier they showed earlier is practically gone. Nothing left but a barren plateau. Looks like a fun place for some dirt biking, though, or off-roading. Now they're showing some new pictures of places that need rain. Mt. Kilimanjaro is losing its snowcap. Glaciers in Greenland are melting and falling into the sea. Does this mean that the earth's atmosphere, full of carbon emissions and greenhouse gases, is heating up the planet?

If so, terrific. I'm for anything that'll help those poor little penguins out. Their little chicks look so tiny and defenseless in the cold weather. And if the ice pack in Antarctica is shrinking, that means their moms and dads won't have so far to go when they need something to eat, right?

And while we're on the subject of eating, that guy with the horseshoe mustache is up at the counter again, this time ordering a Quarter Pounder with Cheese. Hey, what do they call a Quarter Pounder with Cheese in France again? I forget, but it's not a Quarter Pounder with Cheese! Ha!

Now, some boring guy in a blue suit is giving some kind of PowerPoint lecture on rising ocean levels and severe tropical storms. Hello! Alert to the obvious: No one likes cold weather!

If they did, they'd put summer vacations in winter! Repeat: No one likes cold weather. Not even penguins.

Can't get McDonald's out of my mind. Might be a good time to fire up the Expedition and head to the nearest drive-thru. I'll leave the TV on to get past this boring guy's part.

You know what this movie really needs?

More penguins.

That sing and dance.

PETER PAN

(1954)

Blades flash in the setting sun. The wind blows and sails flap around two figures as the battle rages in the top rigging of the pirate ship. Peter Pan is young and quick, but his victory is no certain thing. Captain Hook is a wily adversary, with a fire in his heart that will not let him rest until his mortal enemy is subdued. He swings his rapier and growls through his perfect teeth, "Give it up, boy. Can't you see you're finished?"

Peter laughs a hearty laugh. "What's the matter, old man? Getting tired?"

Their blades whiz through the air and clank icily when they hit. "Not at all, m'lad," he says, "but to surrender now will save much time and exertion."

Down on the deck of the pirate ship, Wendy, Michael, and John watch the battle. Wendy's expression is one of deep concern, while her brothers watch the fight with absent, almost glassy expressions. "Peter! Be careful!"

"You heard the lass. Be careful, Peter, or the next slip may be the last for you."

Sailing through the air, Peter uses his dagger to slice through a supporting line, which makes the yardarm on which Hook is standing lurch and shiver. Of all the times he and Hook have struggled and the battles they have fought, today seems different to him. Peter maintains his bravado, in spite of his uneasy feeling. "Who's slipping?" he asks. "You're the one looking a little clumsy, you codfish."

Hook finds his balance and levels his blade at Peter. "Come now, boy, this has really gone far enough. We know each other too well. In fact, it can be said safely that I'm your last friend left."

"With friends like you, Hook, who needs enemies?"

"Peter, please!" Wendy shouts up to him.

He looks down to her. "Tiger Lily and the Indians! What's keeping them?"

"I'm sorry, Peter. They're not coming to rescue you!"

"It's true, m'boy," clucks the pirate. "They've been paid reparations and gotten casino licenses. They've moved to the other side of Neverland and won't ever be coming back."

The green-clad boy jumps higher into the rigging. "The mermaids! The mermaids will help me!"

"Peter, get your adolescent mind off the mermaids for once! They're nothing but arm candy. You're in serious danger."

"When you think of it," says Hook, "how can mermaids help in a fight? Splash a lot? Throw some kelp? Be reasonable, boy."

Peter's anger flashes in his eyes. "How's this for reasonable?"

he says, and takes a swing with his dagger just an inch from the end of Hook's nose.

"Don't do something you'll regret, lad. . . ."

Their blades cruelly clank again. "Tinkerbell! Wendy, where's Tink?"

"She's run off with Mr. Smee," she shouts. "To Greenwich, I think, to see some parade or other. Said they had to 'show their pride,' whatever that may mean."

"Hook!" Peter says. "You're behind this! You want to destroy me and everything in Neverland . . ."

Hook smiles, "Now, now, everyone's time has to come eventually . . ."

Peter looks down to the deck of the ship and sees the pirates, the Lost Boys, and the Darling children all looking up at him. "But I'm the leader of the Lost Boys! I'll never give up! *Kik-oo-cor-ooo-coo-cooo!*"

Peter beats his chest as he crows and flies up from the yardarm. He expects cheers, but there are none to be heard. Down below, everyone just stares at him, as if somehow he is holding them up.

Hook tries to talk in a beguiling voice, but his impatience is beginning to show. "Peter, this has to stop. . . ."

"NEVER!" he shouts.

"Peter, please," says Wendy from below. "For goodness's sake, just *take* the Ritalin. . . ."

FRANKENSTEIN

(1931)

Oblivious to the rain and lightning, the crowd gathers around the door of the burgermeister's office in the town square late that night. Beneath its angry, impatient shouts is a nerve-rending fear. The villagers had never liked the son of the old baron, with his arrogant, patrician ways and clipped British accent. What right did he have to wear such snappy suits when the rest of them wore itchy lederhosen? And now that there are hints he might be up to something, they have all the evidence they need.

The burgermeister does nothing to calm them down. He knows on which side his strudel is buttered. He shouts, "You men with the torches take the north road, you with the pitchforks take the south. We'll meet at the castle and burn them out if we have to . . ."

With angry shouts the crowd mobilizes. In the flickering torchlight, many of their picket signs are visible. "God Hates Science!" "Creepy Lab Nerds Go Home!" "Reanimation is Murder

Backwards!" On the way, the vigilantes flip some hay wagons and set them ablaze, just for the hell of it.

Rumors have abounded regarding the suspicious activities at Castle Frankenstein. The bodies missing from the cemetery, the break-ins at the brain bank, the robbery at Wolfgang's Big & Tall Shoppe—it must all be leading somewhere, but no one knew where. And like responsible people everywhere, when the villagers are faced with something they don't understand, they reach for the pitchforks first and ask questions later, if at all.

In no time they reach the castle and bang on the door. Much to their surprise, the door is answered quickly by the doctor himself, in a spotless white lab coat. He is all smiles—seems ecstatic, in fact, with a weird look in his eyes. "Yes, my good townsfolk, what can I do for you? What brings you out here on such an inhospitable evening?"

"We want to know what you're doing in there!" shouts one villager.

"What evil experiments are you up to?"

The doctor laughs and puffs on one of his thin cigars. "Why, there's nothing evil at all," he says confidently. "I'm merely conducting experiments in the reanimation of necrified tissue."

"Hell, we're in the middle of Germany," someone says. "Where'd you find any black guys?"

The doctor explains, "No, necrified, *necrified*—it means dead."

"Well, excuse *us*, we're just a bunch of dumb villagers."

"Wait a minute. Do you mean you bring dead things back to life?"

"Precisely," the doctor says.

Howls of protest burst from the crowd. They shout that Dr. Frankenstein is a devil, that his work would cause death, destruction, and damnation for everyone.

"What about impressionable teenagers?" someone shouts. "Raising the dead will become the 'cool' thing to do. This will just encourage them to set up crazy labs and start reanimating things themselves!"

"Say, doc," a male villager asks confidentially, "can your treatment be applied to certain *parts* of living people? I've got . . . this *cousin*, see . . . who's having a little trouble, y'know . . . down there . . ."

Another man shouts, "Hey, did my tax dollars go toward this? Did you get any government grants or anything?"

The doctor replies, "No, all privately funded."

The man shrugs and says, "Okay by me," then walks away. The rest of the crowd keeps shouting, making it clear it is *not* okay with them. Such experiments were immoral, unnatural, illegal, unethical, and most certainly a liberal plot to pad the voter rolls and welfare lists.

"Please! Please!" the doctor says, trying to calm the ruckus. "You're only afraid because you don't understand. Give me a minute to explain!"

But the shouts of the crowd keep coming. As they rise in intensity, Dr. Frankenstein realizes he has only one choice. He opens the doors of the castle wide and calls forth the experiment, his life's obsession, his creation. Slowly a tall figure shambles forth from the shadows, stiff from rigor mortis. Its head nods uneasily upon its neck. When it emerges from the doorway and can be seen by all, there is a gasp, then silence.

The creation raises its arm slowly and tries to wave. It gives a smile and a wink. Then, in the rasp of a kindly old grandfather, it says, "There you go again. . . ."

This startles the crowd. "It can talk!" shout a few rioters.

The creature waits a moment, then continues, "Facts are stupid things. . . . Trees cause more pollution than automobiles do. . . . I've often said there's nothing better for the inside of a man than the outside of a horse. . . . I just signed legislation that outlaws Russia. The bombing begins in five minutes."

The crowd stares, their murderous thoughts driven from their minds and replaced with hope and confidence in the future. The creation smiles and nods and tells an old joke about working in Hollywood. The crowd laughs heartily and cheers as the dawn breaks for another morning in Bavaria.

The burgermeister pushes his way to the front of the crowd and confronts the doctor. "Have you any more of these creatures in your lab?"

"Sadly, no," says the doctor.

"Well then," the burgermeister says confidentially, as he leads the doctor out of the crowd's earshot, "what are your ideas on cloning?"

ALIEN
(1979)

RED STATE, AFFLUENT SUBURB WITH LOTS OF LANDSCAPING JOBS TO FILL

In a dimly lit cafeteria in the bowels of the commercial towing vessel *Nostromo*, its crew gathers for a little food and a few laughs before entering cryogenic sleep again. One of them, Executive Officer Kane, has just emerged from sick bay after a mysterious incident with an unknown life form, and is still groggy and shaken. The crew eats their artificial food, which looks vaguely like Rice-A-Roni, and jokes about enjoying real food again. A few smoke cigarettes, because apparently in the future, one of the few places left to enjoy a puff is a few hundred light-years from Earth.

"Good to have you back, Kane," says Chief Engineer Parker, as Kane hungrily stuffs himself. "I was getting tired of covering for you."

"You coverin'?" Technician Brett says. "I was the one coverin'."

"Yeah, but you know what you need to do before you cover for him? Know how to do your own damn job."

Brett groans in protest and pretends to take a swing at Parker.

The lighthearted mood is shattered when Kane begins groaning and grimacing. Soon he screams, gripping the table in pain.

"Kane, what's wrong?" asks Warrant Officer Ripley.

Thrashing violently, Kane clutches at himself while his confused shipmates try and help. They lay him on the table and hold his arms and legs. Suddenly, blood appears on his shirt and Kane screams louder. From his chest emerges a small creature who growls and screeches at everyone, then scurries off the table and out of the room. The crew is shocked.

"What the hell was *that*?" screams Ripley.

"I don't know, but he sure looks like an industrious little fella," says Parker.

"Yeah, did you see how he just ran off to find work to do?" admires Captain Dallas. "Probably the work the rest of you refuse to do."

"We have to catch it," Ripley says urgently. "There's no telling what . . ."

"Can't catch it now," says Dallas resignedly. "Besides, who's going to do Kane's job, now that he's . . . on permanent disability? Let's see how it works out."

"Wait a minute, that thing ain't in the union!" protests Brett.

"Hey, he's only trying to improve his quality of life," says Dallas.

"But," clarifies Parker, "he's not getting a cut of the profits from this trip."

At that, everyone nods in agreement.

That night Dorothy and her friends rest, though not well. In the morning, they walk through the gates of the city of OZ and set off for the castle of the Wicked Witch of the West. There are no crowds to wave them on, nor any help offered by the city guards. The four are very much on their own. Many of the lampposts are decorated with yellow ribbons, though, which ought to count for something. Above the road is stretched a giant banner that reads "Operation Triumphant Goodliness." As she walks beneath it, Dorothy looks up and sees that the other side is printed with the words, "Mission Accomplished."

"Wow, the Wizard puts a lot of faith in us," the Scarecrow says.

"I think what it means," the Woodsman explains, "is that this mission is so fundamentally right that it cannot fail. The very fact that this plan was concocted by the Wizard, on behalf of the good people of OZ, ipso facto means that it is good. So victory is guaranteed. Only an ignoramus or a traitor would think otherwise."

The Donkey agrees, "It's hard to argue with triumphant goodliness. Why, I . . . I . . . I might even go out on a limb and say . . . I'm *for* it. Oh, feel dizzy." He excuses himself and throws up on the side of the road.

But Dorothy has doubts about this mission that won't go away. Why would the Wizard send the four of them against that witch, with no plan of attack, no weapons besides the Woodsman's ax, and no exit strategy? If he is so all-knowing, why didn't he give them some clues about how to defeat the witch? And why does he want her gone in the first place? "Y'know what, fellas? I don't think we know enough about this whole thing," she admits aloud.

"How much do you need to know?" the Woodsman asks. "She's a threat, and that's good enough for me."

"Maybe we let all the pomp and ceremony distract us," she says. "Don't you remember the story about 'The Emperor's New Clothes'?"

"We're talking about a wizard, girlfriend, not an emperor," the Scarecrow points out. "And what would a giant floating head need with clothes anyway? A hat would be a different story."

Now Dorothy is an all-American girl, and deep in the American character is a healthy streak of skepticism. But questioning the Wizard about this mission is taking that skepticism too far, and is unattractive besides for a girl on the cusp of well-developed womanhood. A better plan might have been to take heed of the witch's magic, because the ruby slippers are beginning to buzz again.

Heading west, the four friends walk quietly through the countryside. The Woodsman's Behemoth has been left behind. It would attract undue attention, and besides, when news of their quest was leaked, gas prices went through the roof. The Black & White City may have been a skittish place, but at least it maintained the appearance of security. Out here in the open, they all feel more vulnerable. The sun goes behind the clouds and the wind howls mournfully. Soon the quartet finds itself in a dark forest. The Woodsman can barely contain his urge to hack and saw through all this abundant timber, but his comrades remind him that stealth is absolutely essential now.

A battered sign by the side of the road warns:

> HAUNTED FOREST.
> *I'd turn back if I were you.*

The Donkey quivers and whines, "What do we do? What do we do?"

The Woodsman asks, "Does the Wizard ever follow anyone's advice?"

"No."

"Then we won't either."

They only proceed a few steps before the Spineless Donkey blurts out, "I can't go on! I can't go on!"

"But you agreed to do this," the Woodsman reminds him.

"I know, I voted for it before I voted against it."

"You can't have it both ways."

The Spineless Donkey cranes his neck 180 degrees and says, "Oh, yes, I can."

"So can I!" the Scarecrow says out of the blue. They all wait a few seconds for an explanation, but none comes.

The Donkey stutters, "M-m-m-maybe we can talk to the witch, you know? N-n-negotiate. She can hand over her broomstick and we'll leave her alone."

The Woodsman scoffs, "The time for talking has passed. The Wizard said she's a menace, and that's good enough for me. Besides, would you give up your broomstick just because someone else wanted it?"

"Of course not," says the Donkey indignantly.

"Okay then."

"They'd have to ask very, very nicely."

The Woodsman grinds his teeth loudly but doesn't say anything. Again showing her skeptical streak, which many observers think is becoming quite unattractive, Dorothy says, "I can't help thinking there's something fishy about all this."

"Not you, too?" the Woodsman exclaims. "You've dealt with witches more than any of us."

"And I'm not sure I trust any of them, or the Wizard either. The 'good' witch slapped these slippers on me without even an explanation. I don't care if they are magic, I don't want them. It hurts to walk in them."

Dorothy bends down and tries to unbuckle a slipper. The thing won't budge, but it emits a warning message: "Please do not tamper with the ruby slippers. They are here for your protection." Then to reassert their importance, they buzz on her feet a little more.

This leaves everyone quite astonished. The Scarecrow marvels, "Their magic must be very powerful."

Dorothy's feet say, "Please speak more directly into the slippers."

The Scarecrow repeats what he said. The slippers thank him.

"That settles it," announces Dorothy. "We're going back to that Wizard and ask him some hard questions about this whole crusade of his. Come on." She turns and walks back on the path, but within a few steps she stops short. As the sky darkens and the wind whistles, a sound slowly comes to their ears, a whooping, hooting cry that seems to be coming from all directions. Then, through the trees, they can see something coming at them, flying in flocks from above.

"What is it?" wails the Spineless Donkey. "What are they?"

"Monkeys! Winged monkeys!" yells the Scarecrow. "But how?"

The Woodsman wonders, "Gene splicing? Bioengineering?"

"Avenging angel monkeys!" Dorothy screams. "Now I *know* we're not in Kansas anymore! Aaaah!"

Dorothy tries to run, but there are so many flying monkeys that she and Toto are quickly surrounded. With their barks and shrieks, the monkeys are truly frightening—not like their cute organ-grinder cousins, although they do dress alike. They chase the Donkey and the Scarecrow down the road and knock them around viciously. Prepared to fight, the Woodsman girds his loins—in his case, with real girders—but the swiftly moving monkeys get him off balance and topple him. The raiders are about to grab Dorothy when everything is interrupted by the pop-pop of automatic gunfire.

Crashing through the brush with weapons in hand are a number of little men in camouflage. It's the Munchkin Militia! Suspicious of Dorothy's true intentions, they've been following her quietly since she left Munchkin City, and the appearance of their ancient enemies, the winged monkeys, has brought them out of the shadows. Jeeps with gun mounts roar up the road as mortar rounds convulse the forest. The monkeys fling as much poop as they can, but the Munchkins are well armed and well trained.

In the pandemonium, our friends become separated. The Munchkins almost have the monkeys in retreat, when through the forest come the talking apple trees and the Midnight Creeper Watchdog Attack Vines. These overgrown science fair experiments have been mobilizing the local plant life to protect the haunted forest and now attack from above and below. The Munchkin weaponry cannot hold back the trees, who have stolen fertilizer bombs from their farms for the battle.

And now coming down the hill is a squadron of dreaded Growleywogs, tall and skinny and armed to the teeth. These are followed by teams of mechanical Copperbottoms, whose clockwork bodies move slowly but unstoppably like armored tanks. Then from the ravine emerges a horde of suicide Winkies. These green-skinned villains run into the crowd and detonate themselves in an effort to prove how peace loving they are.

And in the ensuing chaos of battle among these old and bitter enemies, no one sees Dorothy and Toto being hoisted in the air and flown away.

continued on page 152

DUMBO

(1941)

RED STATE

On a desolate street walk a dejected pair. One, an elephant with huge ears and a sweet baby face, the other a talkative mouse.

"Don't worry, Dumbo, old pal," says the mouse. "You're not in this alone. I'll figure somethin' out for us or my name isn't Timothy Mouse, campaign consultant."

Dumbo gives him a silent smile—oh, but he has such a nice smile!—but inside the elephant is very sad. He and Timothy have lost so many times now, after all. He's beginning to think they'll never manage to win.

As they walk down the road with their tails between their legs, they pass a large live oak tree. And in that tree, on a high branch, sit three black crows. The sight that is passing before them—the elephant with the big ears, and the little mouse with the briefcase, binders, and BlackBerry—is so curious, they need to fly down and get a closer look at it.

"Hey, check dis out," one crow says.

"This is most irregular," says another.

"Hey, homey, goin' somewhere?"

"I ain't yer homey," Timothy says, "and if it's any of yer business, we're headed off to another campaign rally."

"Campaign rally?" say the crows all at once, incredulously.

"With ears like dat?"

"And dat sweet little expression on his face?"

Timothy Mouse gets visibly steamed from this disrespect. "What're you tellin' me? That he *shouldn't* run for office? And why not? Why shouldn't this proud, talented son of Africa be elected and soive the people?"

The crows look at them in wide-eyed amazement, then break out into raucous laughter. Timothy and Dumbo don't know what to say. "Son of Africa!" one bird chokes. "Serve de people!" says another. The birds are laughing so hard they can hardly breathe.

"Come on, Dumbo, enough a dese wise boids," Timothy said. "This ain't yer demographic anyway."

"Now, don't take it that way, Brother Mouse," says one crow.

"Naw, man," says another. "We can help you. We see lots of potential here with your man. Y'see, we're sort of political consultants too, ain't we, boys?"

"You know it," say the other crows, winking.

"Now, you both look tired, beaten down. Your man Dumbo here, he ain't makin' much of a splash, is he?"

Timothy defends the two of them by saying, "Dumbo's makin' a big splash. He's gettin' his woid out to people, but he's gotta deal with boids like you, sayin' that because of his background, he can't run as a conservative."

"Aw, he can run in circles for all we care," the top crow says. "But listen to me: your boy won't win here cuz he's too stiff. If Dumbo wants to win here, he needs a little more swagger. He's got to go a little more street."

"Dat's right," chime in the other crows, stifling their giggles.

"That elephant ain't gonna attract anybody around here till he shows a little more soul."

"Whaddya mean? He's got soul! He's been to church picnic after church picnic . . ."

"Preachin' to the choir. You ain't listenin', Brother Mouse. Let's explain it for him, boys."

I seen a key state swing, heard a diamond pinkie ring,
Heard the Senate call its roll,
But I done seen 'bout ever'thing
When I see Republican soul.

I saw a lame duck, he got up and walked,
And a reporter went out to hear the street talk.
I didn't see that, I only heard,
But that's all that counts in de political world. . . .

I seen a message spin, a loss called a win,
And disaster from a little straw poll,
But I done seen 'bout ever'thing
When I see Republican soul—

Bo Sho Ba-da-do-do!
Da Ba Da Ta-ta-ta!

But I done seen 'bout ever'thing
When I see Republican soul!

KING KONG

(1933)

Standing over the corpse of the recently deposed King Kong, a police lieutenant talks with Carl Denham, the promoter who captured the gigantic ape and brought him to New York. "Well, Denham," the lieutenant says, "the airplanes got him."

"Oh no, twasn't the airplanes," says Denham philosophically. "'Twas Beauty killed the Beast."

"Glad to hear it wasn't the airplanes," says another lieutenant nearby, "'cuz the government just cut New York City's Homeland Security funds by forty percent."

"Are you kiddin' me?" says Denham, dumbfounded.

"What, you don't think that Knoxville and Paducah should be protected against giant monkeys?"

Denham sputters, as only men in tuxedos in Depression-era movies can, "What . . . you mean . . . . aaaah, *nuts*!" before he walks away.

WHEN HARRY MET SALLY

(1989)

In the noise of the busy diner, Harry can't believe his ears. "What is that supposed to mean?"

Sally replies, "Nothing. It's just that all men are sure it never happened to them, and that most women at one time or another have done it, so you do the math."

Harry asks, a little defensively, "You don't think that I could tell the difference?"

"No."

"Get outta here."

Harry returns to his breakfast, confident that this topic is now moot. Sally, on the other side of the table, gives a little smile and begins breathing heavily. Closing her eyes, she begins to moan, "Ooo . . . Oh . . . Ooo . . ."

Harry is a little concerned. "Are you okay?"

Sally keeps up her moaning, eventually rising to an uncontrollable pitch: "Oh . . . Oh God . . . Ooo Oh God . . . Oh . . . Oh . . . Oh . . . Oh God . . . Oh yeah, right there. Oh! Oh . . . YES YES

YES YES . . . OH! OH! OH! . . . OH GOD!! Oh . . . Oh . . . Huh . . . Huh . . . hmmm . . ."

Sally finishes, looks at Harry, and smiles. As she returns to her meal, Harry looks at her, a little uneasy.

Dining with her husband at a nearby table, an older woman motions the waiter over and tells him, "I'll have what she's having."

"Really?" asks the waiter. "You want a lifestyle based on self-gratification and lust that can become such an addiction that it consumes your every waking moment?"

"Eh?"

"You want to slavishly follow empty feminist promises about sexual liberation and ignore the irrefutable fact that sexuality is a gift from God that should only be enjoyed with your husband in the confines of marriage, and only grudgingly even then?"

"What?"

The agitated waiter's voice reaches a crescendo. "You want to chain yourself to the devilish demands of that pitiless carnal slave-driver, the orgasm?!"

"No, you twisted little man. I want the Denver omelet, like she's having. We've been trying to give you our order for twenty minutes!"

The waiter, chastened and sweating, says, "Oh, pardon me for a second. I'll be right back." He heads off to the back room, slightly doubled over, to put a cold towel on his face.

Her slightly deaf husband asks, "What did he say about 'deviled ham'?"

"Nothing, dear," she sighs.

E.T.
THE EXTRATERRESTRIAL
(1982)

RED STATE

      The din of shovels and pickaxes and the disinterested whisper of the wind are all that can be heard now. The midday sun beats down on the men and boys who toil in the dust together, chained at the ankles. If any of them faint, or injure themselves, or worse, they are dragged off to the side and forgotten. Time is short, much work needs to be done, and there is certainly no shortage of humans to do it.

The current crew is ripping out the streets of a California subdivision that is only a few years old. With pick and shovel, hammer and wheelbarrow, the blacktop is taken out in pieces like a jigsaw puzzle. In the end, this will be returned to grassland, but that natural state is hard to envision just now, with the gray baked earth and rocky debris.

Chained to strangers twice and three times his age, Elliott swings his hammer slowly and clumsily. Weeks in the sun have turned his skin brown, but the flesh of his hands is cracked and painful. He thinks he may have ridden these streets on his bike once, but he's not certain. It seems like such a long time ago, it may never have happened at all. Elliott doesn't know how long he's been on this crew, or when he was separated from his brother Greg and his sister Gertie. The overseers make it a policy to split families for the crews, for obvious practical reasons. Little Gert is probably working a watering detail somewhere. And Greg? No way to know.

THWACKKK! A hickory switch is snapped across the back of Elliott's legs. An overseer must have caught him daydreaming about his family and gave him a painful reminder to get back to work.

But Elliott at times can't keep himself from reminiscing. He remembers his home life before this all happened—before that alien came into his life. Bike rides with friends, fighting with his siblings, pizza and movies on Friday night—it may have been predictably suburban, but there's nothing wrong with that. He'd even believed in ecology, once upon a time.

He thought he'd done the right thing by helping the alien. All he'd wanted to do was be back with his family, and Elliott could sympathize. The waddling little botanists seemed so peaceful, so harmless when they arrived. But as they studied Earth and learned how sick their little castaway had gotten from living here, they began to show their true colors. They said they had to stay and save the people on Earth from themselves, to head off global catastrophe.

The aliens used their advanced knowledge of plant life to change the landscape. They made vines grow at phenomenal rates, so high-tension wires could be toppled and power plants choked off. They caused wildflowers and cattails to grow rapidly to make the roads and highways impassable. They forced trees to topple onto buildings, and prairies to take over farms. And when the people fought to stop the insane plans of these tiny tyrants, the aliens fought back, and put the survivors to work reclaiming the land.

Elliott remembers all of it, and feelings of guilt and sadness and rage have made him a problem worker. He takes a swing at the little alien who just struck him, but misses. An alien on horseback hits him in the head with a rifle butt, and Elliott's skull is nearly fractured. His limp body is unshackled from his gang and dragged up in front of the head man. The aliens talk with each other in their weird, buzzy language. Elliott painfully lifts his head to look at the head man. In a flash, he recognizes him. Even with the mirrored sunglasses and crisp white Stetson, the face is clearly that of the first alien to arrive.

"E.T.," Elliott gasps. "E.T., why did all this have to happen? How can you do this to me?"

The extraterrestrial considers the pitiful boy. He raises his long neck and explains in his cruel croak of a voice, "What we have here is a failure to communicate."

STAR WARS

(1976)

LONG AGO, IN A RED STATE FAR, FAR AWAY

Standing on his Death Star, the technological envy of the galaxy (complete with a missile defense shield that works flawlessly 100 percent of the time), Darth Vader waits for the arrival of his longtime enemy Obi-Wan Kenobi, and Kenobi's young ally, Luke Skywalker. While his intelligence network has alerted him of this development, he can also feel it in his gut. He goes by his gut a lot.

Vader's been threatened by these and their kind before, holdovers stuck in some pathetic hippie-dippie time warp. Whatever their pie-in-the-atmosphere ideals, however, people in a rebellion are by definition rebels, and rebels are a threat to peace and freedom, and must be eradicated by any and all means. For years, Vader has taken the offensive, but the rebels' surprise tactics and complete disregard for human and nonhuman life have given them some quick victories. This, combined with the biased coverage of the mainstream hologram transmitters, has begun to weaken the resolve of everyone around him, who are now busy writing their memoirs to cover their own heat shields. But Vader has fought alone in the past, and he's ready to do it again.

Obi-Wan, a purveyor of squishy Eastern claptrap, has acquired a following of young, impressionable acolytes with his nonsense. Vader knows the responsibilities of running a galaxy require a more adult frame of mind. One of his favorite books is Sidious's best seller, *The 7-Minute Tyrant*. The little people have to be protected, after all, and someone needs to make the transport modules run on time.

When they arrive, Lord Vader is ready. He's not one to shy from battle or make decisions long distance from the safety of a drone battleship. Obi-Wan is the first to draw his light saber.

"It's been a long time, old man," says Vader. "You are weak."

"I sense the Force is not as strong with you, Vader, as you would have others believe."

"As a wise man once said, you go into battle with the Force you have, not the Force you might want or wish to have at a later time."

After more trash talk and propaganda, the battle begins. Their light sabers buzz and crack in the air like amplified bug lamps. Within minutes, the fight is over, and Vader topples Obi-Wan with a smashing blow.

Luke and his rebel pals try and escape the ship, scurrying to hide themselves among the general population, but Vader is prepared and cuts them off. The boy tries to gain sympathy with a sob story about growing up with a foster family on a planet so poor and desolate that the only thing they had to farm was moisture.

Abandoned by his father as he was, he had no choice but to become a rebel.

This sniveling moves Vader not at all. Adversity builds character, he reminds the rebel. In their light-saber duel, Vader has Luke at his mercy until he is rescued by his sister, Leia the Lesbian Librarian. (It's a sign of this rebellion's perverse and vile nature that brother and sister would toy with romantic involvement, even considering Leia's sexual confusion.) She's a formidable foe, far tougher than her brother, and Vader has a personal code not to hit girls, even big ones. After distracting her with piped-in folk music, Vader eventually defeats her and sends her to a reeducation camp at a Baptist college.

Vader is unsure of whether to reveal to Luke that he is in fact his father, as it is sure to embarrass him in later hearings in front of the Senate. Instead, he buys Luke off by granting him dominion over some of the Banana Planets on the edge of the galaxy, thus restoring order to the Galactic Empire once more.

THE WIZARD OF DUBYA

(1939)

PART SIX

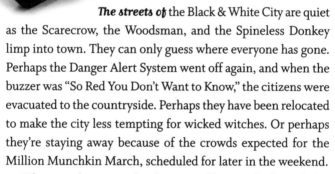

The streets of the Black & White City are quiet as the Scarecrow, the Woodsman, and the Spineless Donkey limp into town. They can only guess where everyone has gone. Perhaps the Danger Alert System went off again, and when the buzzer was "So Red You Don't Want to Know," the citizens were evacuated to the countryside. Perhaps they have been relocated to make the city less tempting for wicked witches. Or perhaps they're staying away because of the crowds expected for the Million Munchkin March, scheduled for later in the weekend.

Whatever the cause, the three are able to walk through the city unseen and unheralded. Even the palace guards are nowhere around. The eerie silence would have unnerved the trio, had they not been so exhausted from the battle they just survived.

Before their trip here and the mission given by the Wizard, they'd never dreamed they'd see such carnage. Weighing heaviest on their hearts is the fate of poor Dorothy. When she was taken, they assumed the filthy airborne primates had been sent by the Wicked Witch. But as the conflict escalated and more groups dove in, this became less clear. The Scarecrow, the Donkey, and the Woodsman were lucky to escape with their lives. Now they could only imagine what kind of petting zoo Dorothy had been carried off to.

As they make their way closer to the palace of the Wizard, the silence gradually gives way to the noise of construction. Trucks, cement mixers, hammering, sawing—in the near vicinity of the palace the clamor is deafening. The haggard three try to find their way to the portal of the palace, but so many changes are being made to everything that their heads are spinning. The façade of the building, which had been so austere and imposing, is now covered with buzzing neon and flashing lights. In the plaza is an elaborate, computer-controlled fountain with a simulated erupting volcano. Where the guard had once blocked their way, there's now a portico and a wide red carpet, with doormen and bellboys standing ready in the circular driveway.

Above the portico was a large marquee inviting people to the Golden Dragon Hotel and Casino, a division of Jenk-Stonings, Inc.

"Things move so fast these days," mutters the Woodsman.

The Scarecrow looks around at the crowds streaming into the casino's main lobby. They look nothing like the worried citizens he'd seen only the day before. These are well-dressed visitors from all over OZ, happy and laughing, with plenty of money to spread around. "Well," he says dejectedly to his friends, "let's go in and get this over with."

Inside the garish lobby they are able to walk where they want without being stopped. The patrons are so intent on merrymaking that the bedraggled trio goes unnoticed. Still, there are hidden cameras everywhere, so the Scarecrow, the Donkey, and the Woodsman know they will be spotted soon if they aren't careful. They sneak to one side, walk behind a massive row of slot machines, and duck into a small room.

What they'd thought was a quiet hideout, however, is a small nightclub, with candles on the tables and cocktail waitresses carrying trays of drinks to pickled customers. Onstage was a big elderly woman with white hair, wearing pearls and a navy-blue dress. She had the look of a doting grandmother, the swagger of a sailor, and the mouth of an insult comedian.

"Hey, those sonsabitches were poor as dirt before the buses came in and rescued their sorry asses," the comedian says, "and in the end, they get a free bus trip to the big city, some bottled water, and K-rations. I think it worked out pretty well for them in the end. Maybe next time, they'll think twice before they live someplace that's *below sea level*! Haha! Am I right?"

This abusive type of entertainment repulses our friends, so they leave that room and search out another. What they think might be the door to the Wizard's chamber only leads to another nightclub, where a hunched-over old man is performing sharpshooter tricks onstage with a shotgun. "Come on," the old man growls at the audience out of the side of his mouth, "all I need's one volunteer for this trick. This one's a humdinger. Forget what happened last time."

"I want to get out of here," the Donkey says. "There's something very wrong going on."

"Let's try one more room," says the Woodsman.

The last room they enter is a little bigger than the other two, with a large, bright stage, a shimmery silver curtain, and a small orchestra in dinner jackets. Even the Scarecrow, whose tastes tend to be a bit outlandish, thinks the music is brassy, corny, and over the top. They spend some time in the crowded room before they can tell who is on stage, but by the time they do, they wish they hadn't.

The Spineless Donkey whispers to the Woodsman, "Hey, who's that worn-out-looking singer up there?"

The Woodsman squints his eyes and grits his teeth. "That's Dorothy."

She is dressed in a low-cut black gingham evening gown and is singing in a husky warble that belies her young years, but the singer onstage is definitely Dorothy, belting out torch songs about spoiled love affairs and sentimental disillusionment. On the piano next to her is a framed portrait of little Toto. Whatever had turned her from an energetic young girl into this battered spectacle, the three friends can't stomach watching her up there, baring her soul and legs in front of a bunch of drunken conventioneers. The three climb onstage, and the Woodsman stands guard with his ax while the Donkey and the Scarecrow pick Dorothy up and carry her off.

The foursome run through a maze of service hallways, trying to find a safe place to stop. Dorothy seems in a daze and barely recognizes the friends she knew only the day before. Try as they might, they can find no more hiding places. Their only chance is to find a way out of the casino.

"This way," says the Woodsman, consulting his onboard GPS screen. "The exit should be over this way." But the harder they try to find the way out, the farther into the casino they go. As they pass their seventh Golden Dragon souvenir stand, they come face to face—or rather, head-to-head—with the all-powerful, all-knowing Wizard of Dubya! Fear freezes them in their steps. They have no idea what he'll do to them for their failure to get the witch's broomstick, let alone snatching Dorothy offstage in the middle of her act.

Will he blast them with fire balls? Will he turn them into statues? Will he exile them to the burning wastelands? Hard to say. Somehow, the grandeur and majesty of the Wizard have been taken down a peg by the sight of the floating head working as a greeter in the hotel.

"Hi . . . hey there . . . welcome to the casino, glad to have ya," the Wizard says to different people passing through the spacious lobby. When he sees Dorothy and her friends, instead of getting angry, he remains all smiles. "Well, look who's here. Hay Bale, Chopper Dude, and the Burrito. How y'all doin'? Is Dotty on break?"

The Scarecrow is the first one who can manage to spit out a question. "What . . . what are you doing here, in the middle of the lobby? What's happened here? Aren't you the all-powerful Wizard any more?"

"Those are good questions, heh-heh. Nothin' gets past you, huh? Heh-heh. Did you fellas check out the free buffet in the Szechuan Room? Great pot stickers." Then he turned his head, still floating lighter than air, toward another group of guests arriving at the casino.

"Wait a minute!" the Scarecrow howls. "We need some answers."

The Woodsman growls, "You send us out on a dangerous mission and then you tell us to try the pot stickers!? That won't cut it!"

"Yeah," the Donkey says, "no matter how good they are."

The head floats back to them, with a smirk on his face that seems comradely, confidential, and contemptuous all at the same time. "Your mission was dangerous. It was vital to our continued security. You faced an implacable enemy, one that needed a good placcing. You did your best, and so did we. And the best we can do is the best. I know better than anyone, intelligence can't always be relied. On. But history will vindicate us. You watch."

"And what about Dorothy?" the Scarecrow asks. "What the hell happened to her?" At the mention of her name, Dorothy tries to break out of her swoon.

"Now, y'all have to realize, there are certain things that can't be discussed. Much as I'd like to, but in the interests of security, we can't. It would embolden the enemy. . . ."

"You sent the monkeys, didn't you?" the Woodsman yells. "And the slippers, too!"

A pair of tourists comes up and a woman excitedly asks, "We're sorry to interrupt, but did we hear you say slippers? We came all the way from Rinkitink to see the ruby slippers, along with the Toto Memorial. Where are they?"

The Wizard smiles and says, "Mezzanine level, just past the Baccarat Room."

As they walk away, the woman says to her husband, "They say the stuffed Toto looks so lifelike, it's just like the real thing."

The Scarecrow yells, "What's going on?"

"I can't discuss ongoing operations," says the Wizard testily. "I will say that we questioned Dorothy within the limits of the law, and she gave up some vital information about the threat posed by this place Kansas, about their capability of launching more farmhouses, barns, and even whole ranches in our direction. OZ is now safer because of this information."

"You . . . what?" the Woodsman sputters.

"But she's such a young gal, we decided to give her a chance to redeem herself. She was probably brainwarshed at a young age. But she's a heckuva singer, don't you think? She's a big draw here. Now, I insist, you really must go try the pot stickers. . . ."

As he was saying this, two large men in sharkskin suits came up from behind. "What's going on, fellas?" one said. "Please don't interfere with employees while they're working."

The Scarecrow and Donkey don't quite know what to do, but the Woodsman says, "Shove it, pal. Dorothy's no employee here, she's just a girl who trusted this Wizard to do the right thing and keep his word. Now look at her."

The other man ignores him and says, "C'mon, Dorothy, time for your next number." As the men try and take Dorothy by the arm, the Woodsman raises his ax. Before he can stop them, a little old woman inserts her "Winner's Circle" club card into his back and tries to use him as a slot machine. With his electrical system shorted out, the brave Woodsman is paralyzed.

The men start to pull Dorothy away, but the Scarecrow and Donkey grab her arm and pull her back. More security men rush over, and a desperate tug-of-war begins. Poor Dorothy is pulled back and forth between them, barely conscious until she starts to mutter, over and over, "There's no place like home, there's no place like home. . . ."

As she says these words, the casino lobby spins all around her. Images of her adventures—the tornado, the Munchkins, the witches, and her three dear friends—flash before Dorothy's mind. She blacks out for a moment, then awakes. When she does, she finds she's right back where she started.

Backstage at the Golden Dragon Hotel and Casino, waiting to go on for her next show.

RECUTS IN DEVELOPMENT

RED STATES

ON THE WATERBOARD

RAIDERS OF THE LOST IRAQI NATIONAL MUSEUM

FROM HERE TO APOCALYPSE TO ETERNITY

DECIDER HOUSE RULES

ROVEHEART

DAS SWIFT BOOT

KILL BILL (AND HILLARY, WHILE YOU'RE AT IT)

SOME LIKE IT HOT, BUT DON'T ADMIT IT

SATURDAY NIGHT FEMA

BLUE STATES

THE PASSION OF THE TENURED HUMANIST PHILOSOPHER

GHOST-FILIBUSTERS

THE HEALTHY BREAKFAST CLUB

RAISING ARIZONA TAKES A VILLAGE

MUTUAL INTERDEPENDENCE DAY

THE PRINCE BRIDE

FOUR COMMITMENT CEREMONIES AND A FUNERAL

ONE FLEW OVER THE REHAB FACILITY

THE DEER CATCHER-RELEASER

NANOOK OF THE ARCTIC NATIONAL WILDLIFE RESERVE

RED STATES	*BLUE STATES*
North by North Korea	*The Commitments, or Lack Thereof*
Lame Duck Soup	*Who Cloned Roger Rabbit?*
Murder by Death Tax	*Take the Money and Cut and Run*
New Jack Abramoff City	*Willy Policy Wonka*
All About Adam and Eve	*Commie Dearest*
A Day at the Race-Baitings	*A Fistful of Dollars the Government Knows How to Spend Better Than You*
The Nutty Provisional Authority	*Class War of the Worlds*
The Sunni Also Rises	*White Men Can't Jump All Over the Constitution*
How Green Was My Green Zone	*Inherit the Deficit*
Saving Private Retirement Accounts	*Twelve Angry Special Interest Groups*
Good Will Squandering	*Wild Organic Strawberries*
Touch of Axis of Evil	*The Polarized Express*
Mission Impossible Accomplished	*The Woman Who Knew Too Much and Wasn't Afraid to Show It*
Old Yeller Cake	*Dial M for Mass Transit*
Gone with the WMDs	*To Rehabilitate a Thief*
Nationalistic Velvet	*The Seventh Baby Harp Seal*

RED STATES

Honey, I Shrunk Our International Standing

Terminator 3: Rise of the Voting Machines

Halliburton Is for Heroes

Phantom of the Grand Ole Opry

House Page Party

A Streetcar Named Abstinence

Shock and Jaws

The Day the Earth Warmed Up

BLUE STATES

The French Connection to Superior Living

Barack to the Future

2 Fast 2 Furious 4 a Hybrid

Beach Station Zebra

As Good as It's Ever Going to Get, and Probably Not Even That